BEEF
STEW
FOR THE MIND

MJ Wilson

ISBN:0692387773
ISBN:9780692387771

Person One isn't paying attention and falls into a deep pit.

Person Two follows, believing it's what Person One intended.

Person Three runs to the pit, jumps in and proclaims to the others, *"Life IS a deep pit we all must endure, so let's make the best of it."*

Person Four stands outside the pit and says, *"Maybe we should try another way."*

I say we go with Person Four.

-MJ Wilson

DEDICATION

This book* is dedicated to all the single moms in the world who give everything they've got, *every day*, to make the best life possible for their children. I hope and pray you not only find the peace, love and rest, you so rightly deserve, but that the stories in this book will somehow inspire, encourage, entertain, and even give you a bit of an escape in the middle of an otherwise very busy day.

-MJ Wilson

P.S. – Be sure to read *The Real Wonder Woman* – I know you'll identify with it!

---

* A portion of the proceeds from this book will go to support single moms with living expenses such as rent, food, school supplies and clothing. (If you'd like to donate directly, please visit MJ-Wilson.com)

CONTENTS

MJ WILSON

NOTE TO THE READER

Although the stories within this book were inspired by real events, none of them are based upon one specific event, organization, person or group of people. These stories are illustrative examples only. *Any resemblance to real persons, living or dead, is purely coincidental.* All locations and names have been fictionalized (other than my own), and regardless of what anyone may think, none of these stories are transparent attempts to publicly praise or mock my friends, their enemies (or mine!) or exes. (However, several of my friends certainly wanted me to!)

-MJ Wilson

INTRODUCTION

This book is not an "Answer Key" and the stories I've written are not given to you as the solutions themselves. (Think of them more like possibilities and I believe we'll be on the same page.) The purpose of this book is to get you to *think*. Think about your life and how you're handling it.

You've probably heard what's usually referred to as the Golden Rule: "Do unto others as you'd have others do unto you." That's certainly a great rule to live by. But have we become so accustomed to this Golden Rule mindset (whether we actually live by it or not) that while we're "doing unto others" we've stopped looking at what others are doing to us? Or what we're doing to ourselves?

It's something to think about, and that's exactly what I want you to do … *think about it.*

Take a serious look at your way of life – your job, relationships, beliefs, customs – and ask, "Is *my* life working? Is this all there is or should I expect more?" (And just to be fair, consider this: If your way of life *is* working, that doesn't necessarily mean it works for everyone. It might just mean it works for you – *and possibly at the expense of others.)*

Keeping this in mind, will you do me a small favor? Before you dive into the first story, will you *please* – regardless of your beliefs, traditions and viewpoints – open your mind, prepare your heart and listen with both? With so many of us feeling unhappy with our jobs or relationships, fighting depression and sickness, sinking further into debt, or simply settling for a life that's less than what we deserve or want, perhaps it's time we consider trying something different.

Something beyond what we've always done in the past.

Something … *new*.

My chemistry professor used to say, "Change one variable of the experiment and you change the entire outcome and results."

I think it's time we change a variable … *or two*.

-MJ Wilson

Sex With The Ex

*You can't overcome the pain
if you keep letting the pain come over*

I know my commitment to Josh was quick, but I was socially tired, emotionally exhausted and physically lonely. He just seemed to say all the right things at all the right times. We really hit it off – until he did it.

"Did what?" you ask?

Did what every man does who "did it" to his girl: He cheated on me.

It was the night of my 23rd birthday. He was supposed to pick me up at 8 o'clock to take me to my favorite restaurant and give me my gift. Afterwards we had plans to go back to my place for some "dessert." However, even though it was *my* birthday, I wanted to surprise him as well and give him a gift, too. I wanted to show him how much I appreciated him. (I bought him two tickets to see his favorite comedian who was going to be in town next month. I figured we could both enjoy a nice, fun evening out.)

So how'd it all go down? I showed up at his place two hours before he was supposed to be at mine, tickets in hand, only to find his ex-girlfriend's car parked outside, his front door slightly open and his clothes, as well as hers, all over the floor. I walked halfway up the stairs hearing what sounded to me like two people having sex. Now technically I didn't see anything. That bedroom door was shut and I wasn't about to open it. I just couldn't handle what I might see on the other side if I did. But, I did hear a lot of heavy breathing and moaning and that was enough for me.

I was so hurt I just ran out of there. Neither of them even realized I had been there until they heard the screen door slam shut and my car tires screeching out of the apartment complex. I was devastated.

He called and texted a million times within the next 20 minutes, but I never answered. Within the hour, he showed up at my front door, begging me to let him explain. I didn't want to, but he said he wouldn't go away until I did. So I let him in. (I know … bad idea.)

Basically he said it wasn't his fault. He said Alyssa (his ex) had shown up unannounced and took him by surprise. BUT, he swore up and down nothing actually happened. He said she kept trying to get him to have sex with her but he wouldn't. He told me what I heard was him wrestling to get her off him.

I didn't really believe him. Okay, I didn't believe him at all. But I really wanted to. My heart was aching and *the only person I wanted to seek refuge in was the very person I needed refuge from.* (You ever had *that* problem?) I know it sounds crazy, but I needed his story to be true so I could have a little peace of mind. Besides, I really *didn't* see anything. What if he was telling me the truth?

After 45-minutes of listening to him apologize and beg, I told him I believed him and we made up. The rest of the evening went just as planned (minus the dessert, of course – I wasn't about to have sex with him the same night) and all was well. We continued dating as if nothing had ever happened. Life was good and seemingly getting better. However, just three weeks later he texted me and told me he felt he rushed into things and now wanted to take a break for a little while. Said he needed "some space."

Space?

What the hell does that mean?

Space so you can think? Space so you can work on your career? Or space so you can screw another girl?

I was crushed. *Again.*

I told him to do whatever he wanted, just leave me alone. I was done with him and didn't want to see him anymore.

So he did … for the next two months.

At 12:22 a.m. on a Friday night … no wait … "Saturday morning" technically, I'm lying in my bed half asleep, when my phone suddenly notifies me I have a text. Now you and I both know – there are only two types of texts any girl gets after midnight: emergencies and booty calls. And which do you think I got?

"Hey ma – How u been? R u up?" was the text.

"I'm in bed. What do u want?" I texted back, knowing full well what Josh wanted.

"I'm outside. Can I come in? I wanna talk."

Now this is the part every girl hates – and loves – at the same time. Why do we hate it? Because no girl wants to feel used or controlled, especially by a man she doesn't trust anymore. And although I suppose I'll never know if Josh actually cheated on me, one thing was for sure: I didn't trust him anymore.

Why do we love it? Because every girl wants to be wanted … even if she doesn't want the guy back. So, strange as it may sound, although I knew I didn't want Josh, I knew Josh wanted me, and that made me feel good. Almost as if I were now in control. So … I let him come in.

I'd like to say that we had a great talk and worked things out. Or better yet, that I didn't need him anymore and told him to leave. But the truth is, I was lonely. And I did miss him a little. So I let him stay over.

No commitment. No exclusive relationship. Just two adults sharing each other's company, bed and ... well ... *you know.*

This went off and on for the next three months. Loved being wanted, hated feeling used. I knew something had to change and that something was me. But how? How do I break the cycle?

I finally shared my situation – and a couple bottles of wine! – with my best friend, Jessica. I was hoping to forget about Josh, if only for a night, and feel like somebody understood how I felt.

After we had a few drinks (okay ... MANY drinks) and plenty of female venting, Jessica said something that totally changed my entire perspective ... Probably been said a million times, yet it was the first time I'd ever heard it myself:

"Ex-boyfriends and ex-girlfriends are exes for a reason."

She said something else after that but my mind drowned it out. "That is so true" I thought to myself, and immediately began to think about every reason why Josh was my ex. The more I thought, the angrier I got. The angrier I got, the stronger I became. I rehearsed this process over and over for the next few days, preparing myself for Josh's next offer to "talk" after midnight. But unfortunately, that offer never came. Apparently, he had found someone new.

Go figure.

A few months went by and I met Michael – my new man and definite love of my life! He works at the local hospital with Jessica. She introduced us at her birthday bash a while back and we've been together ever since. *He is amazing.* He's 26, never been married, and works as a physician's assistant. He loves his mother, became the legal guardian of his niece after his sister passed due to cancer, and is an all around good guy. (He even brought me flowers on our first date and opened my car door! I didn't think men did that anymore! Am I lucky or what?)

So kind. So considerate. So … *Michael.* (God I love him!) It's amazing what having the right person in your life can do for you. Makes me so glad I didn't settle for being Josh's "Plan B."

Six months into our relationship, and slightly after midnight again (just as we're getting into bed), my phone notifies me I have another text. Now at this point it's been nearly eight months since I've seen or heard from Josh. It never crossed my mind it might be him. But as I picked up my phone and looked at the number (I had deleted his name from my contacts already) I knew exactly who it was and exactly what he wanted.

"Hey ma – How u been? R u up?" his text read.

But this time, instead of texting him back, I called his phone. I wanted the satisfaction of telling him off myself. When he answered, he immediately gave me his typical speech: "I'm outside. Can I come in? I wanna talk." But before I could answer, Michael rolled over and said, "Baby who you talkin' to?" He said it loud enough for Josh to hear, which freaked Josh out.

"WHO'S THAT?" Josh asked.

I said, "That's my boyfriend. He wants to know who's on the phone."

"Tell him JOSHUA IS ON THE PHONE if he wants to know so bad."

So I did. And before I could say another word, Michael grabbed the phone outta my hand and in a very sarcastic, aggressive tone said, "Nice to meet you, Joshua – 'man on the phone'. I'm Michael – 'man in the bed.' Now f*ck off." And then hung up.

WHOOOOOOOO! GOD I LOVE MY MAN! Nothing better than having your knight in shining armor come to your rescue! (Makes me love Michael that much more!)

Okay, okay … I gotta be honest. I hate to admit it, but that's not really what happened. (Although I've pictured it like that a thousand times in my mind. Kind of like the way they do In the movies when people daydream about how they want their story to end. I think it would've been hilarious.) Anyway, it didn't go down quite like that. Michael's not that kind of man. He's not on Josh's immature level – he's far above it. And although I'm sure if I had asked Michael to handle the situation he would have, deep down I needed to handle it myself. I had been putting up with Josh in my life all this time because I didn't have someone like Michael in it … and it shouldn't have been that way. Waiting for a good man to come into my life before telling a bad one to leave had cost me long enough.

(*Oh ladies … go back and read that line again and again and let that lesson sink in, please!*)

I was ready to move forward and this was my chance.

So, as I was saying, Josh actually did text me. And Michael really was there. But Michael had already fallen asleep on the couch and I was still up working on a project for work. So when I got Josh's text I took the opportunity to do what I should've done a long time ago:

I told Josh goodbye.

For good.

I texted him back and told him to meet me out front. I wanted to tell him in person exactly how I felt.

As soon as he saw me he came with all that, "Hey baby … how you been?" crap as if he was just gonna waltz right back into my life like he had never left. I immediately replied.

"FIRST OF ALL, I'm not your baby.

SECOND, I've never been better.

AND THIRD, I have finally come to a clear understanding of what you and I were and currently are …

ONE.
HUGE.
MISTAKE."

I then proceeded to share with him a little about my new-found love for Michael and how much happier I am now that I've not only found a man who sees and values my worth, but more importantly, that I see it and value it, too.

With that, I told him goodbye. No anger. No "eff you" type of attitude. Just a "thanks, but no thanks and goodbye" type of ending.

Why? Because Josh was the a**hole, not me. And I refused to become what he was (and probably still is) simply to communicate to him how I felt. He had his chance. And now it's gone.

I'm a better woman now. I'm a happier woman now. And I'm a complete woman now. Not because I found Michael, *but because I found myself*. Not only do I see my own value, but I now know what values to look for in others.

Jessica was right. Josh *is* my ex for a reason. And Michael – the only man worthy of my love – he's the *only* man I'm pleasin'.

-Ashley / Chicago, IL

The Problem With Your Problems

If you want others to mind their business,
you're going to have to mind your garden

"Why do people cause so much drama in my life?"

"Why is everyone so obsessed with *every* little thing I do?"

"Why can't they just worry about themselves and leave me alone?"

If you find yourself asking these questions, I suggest you take a look at yourself and the people you allow into your life. Just because they're in your world doesn't mean they need to be in your circle.

Be careful …

Weeds and flowers grow in the same soil.

Knowing which to cut out and which to let bloom … *that's* what matters.

-MJ Wilson

The *Real* Wonder Woman

All parents have children,
but not all children have parents

As a single mother, between working full-time, taking my daughter to daycare or my son to ball practice, helping with homework, fixing (a late) dinner, doing the dishes, and making sure everyone's gotten a bath and tucked in, "free time" isn't exactly something I'm familiar with. By the time I make sure everyone else's world is safe and secure, it's easily 10 p.m. (or later) and I, for the first time "today" (if you still wanna call it a day) am just now starting *my* day.

What shall I do? Catch up on one of my 12 prerecorded episodes of *Dateline* or *Dr. Oz*? Maybe grab a glass of wine, light a few candles and relax in a hot bath? Oh wait … How about I actually go to bed early and get a little extra sleep? No. Forget that. Then I lose all my free time and I'm starting all over again tomorrow as soon as I wake up.

So what do I do? (I know, I know … it's only an extra hour or so at best, but hey, I'll take any free time I can get, so I don't wanna waste it.)

(Thinking …)

Of course! I know exactly what I'll do. The same thing all of us hard-working / talented / often-forgotten / sometimes-looked-down-upon / put-our-kids-first-and-commit-to-give-them-a-better-

life-than-we-had / it's-not-about-me-right- now-it's-about-them /
single parents do:

LAUNDRY!

Now if you're not a parent, or if you are but have the help of a
spouse, you might not understand why I would choose to spend
my free time doing the laundry, when I could be doing so many
other things. So please, allow me to explain.

I don't have the luxury of another spouse's help in my home – not
with finances, discipline, homework, ball practice, cleaning or
about a million other things I'd list, but I don't have the time to do
that because I have to do the laundry, remember? And in case
you're wondering, I didn't "ask for this" either – as if any of us do.
My babies' father and I were married at one time and it was
beautiful. But just after I informed him we were about to have our
second child, he informed me he was having an affair and wanted
out of our marriage. He left two months before our daughter was
born. And never came back.

Due to this reality, the bottom line is, if something needs done
around here and I don't do it, it doesn't get done. Period. Now
granted, my kids can help ... eventually. But having an 8-year-old
and a 3-year-old doesn't exactly make two employees for my
benefit. And although my oldest one is more than willing to help
(he's such a "Mama's boy"), and often does, by the time we get
the essentials done (school, practice, dinner, homework, bath) it's
time for bed. So that leaves just me, and knowing that, you may
think the reason I choose to do laundry now, during the only free
time I get, is because I don't want a mess to clean up in the
morning or because I want to stay on top of things so they don't
get out of hand. And to a small extent, that's true. But the overall
reason is far, far greater.

The reason I, and so many other single parents just like me,
choose to spend our free time doing the laundry (or the dishes, or
something similar) when there are so many other things we'd
rather do with our time, is because *we are making an investment
into the lives of our children*. When my little boy Jayden and my
baby girl Layla wake up in the morning, they are not going to wake

up to a home that is a mess, lacking structure and discipline. They will wake up tomorrow – as they have every day since their father left – to a home that is clean, safe and beneficial to their livelihood. One that represents pride, respect, possibility, integrity, dignity, and even hope.

"Hope?" you ask. Yes, *hope*.

You see, it's not just a home to them (whether they realize it or not, at the moment). It's a representation of who they are ... who **WE** are.

We do NOT lie down when the odds are against us, we do NOT give in to despair when the world expects us to, we do NOT become "less than" simply because we have less, and we damn sure do NOT make excuses of why we cannot succeed or be at our best because of who left or why. Whether Jayden's kicking a soccer ball, Layla's learning her alphabet or I'm taking online courses to improve my education, we do it, ALL OF IT, with excellence. And the fact that my ex-husband and their father walked out on us when we needed him the most, only makes me even that much more determined to succeed.

I refuse to be less than what I can be as a mother, simply because he's chosen to be less than he should be as a father.

So, no ... I will not watch my shows tonight. No ... I will not take a hot bath. And no, I will not go to bed early. Hell, I won't even speak poorly about their father to them. What I will do, however, *is the laundry* – OUR laundry, keeping this house as clean as a two-parent home ... and I will keep investing in my children's lives. Because when they're old enough to finally realize what their father has done *to them*, instead of hating him and the world they live in because of it, they will also be old enough to realize what their mother has done *for them*, and in doing so, they will fight that much harder for what is theirs – a life full of love, happiness, and yes ... even hope.

-Kesha / Charleston, SC

Because I Said So, *That's* Why

You can't control the speed of the rollercoaster,
or the height of the hill, but you <u>can</u> decide
if you choose to ride

_____

Whether you're 28 or 88, once you're an adult, you're an adult. You don't have to wait until you reach a certain age or obtain a certain status to begin to say no to things you just don't want to do or be a part of. A simple "No" will do, and if anyone asks why, just say, "Because I said so, that's why."

The following is a list of several things that I absolve you from being a part of, anytime, anyplace, should you prefer to. And please notice I said, "should you prefer to." If you desire to be a part of any of the following, that's certainly up to you.

1. **Any management position**
    (Definition of a manager: person who has to deal with everyone's sh*t, yet doesn't get paid nearly enough for doing so.)

2. **New clothing styles**
    (Live long enough and it all comes back around anyway ... trust me.)

3. **Any non-mandatory event scheduled to take place before 10 a.m.**
    (What could possibly be so important so early that couldn't

happen after a nice lunch?)

4. **Any outing that involves bug spray**
(If you have to spray something *on you* to keep something off ...)

5. **Theme Parks**
(What's wrong with a regular park? Why do you need a theme? Go for a walk instead. It's cheaper and better for your heart.)

6. **Any sporting event you don't give a damn about**
(Who cares if the whole town shuts down when the local team plays? Unless that team is paying your rent, you don't have to go!)

7. **Office Parties / Christmas Parties**
(Insert yawn here.)

8. **Birthday Parties**
(Yes, the individual *does* matter, but your attendance won't if you just send cash ☺)

9. **Local festivals that charge more money for parking than entering**
(However, you may want to sneak your kid in long enough to bring back some funnel cakes! *Yuuuuummmmmy!*)

10. **Any movie with the number 2 in its title**
(You and I both know they're never as good as the first. Just rent or buy it later and spare yourself the $15 for a *small* cola.)

11. **Any diet that doesn't allow coffee or chocolate**
(WTH?)

12. **Dinner dates with other couples**
(Do I have to explain this one?)

13. **Expensive church services**
(If they got a cover charge – aka "love offering" – when you

enter and three more offerings before you leave ...)

14. Reunions
(Thanks to Facebook, you already know who's divorced, how fat they are, and their favorite TV show.)

15. Weddings
(Especially if there's A LOT of singing during the ceremony and no open bar at the reception!)

16. Major family vacations
(If your family vacation requires an agenda, meeting times and a budget, it's not a vacation – *it's a second job.* Stay home and play ball with the kids in the backyard instead. Not only is it cheaper, but it's also an ancient ritual called "being a family.")

17. Conferences for your job
(Unless they're two or more hours away and in a really cool city, they're just an extended version of your already annoying job.)

18. Baby Showers
(See "Birthday Parties" listed previously)

19. Sleeping accommodations
(Don't believe the hype – a "pull-out couch" is *NOT* a bed!)

20. "Chipping in" at the office for a stupid gift
(Stop throwing your money away on people you wouldn't even go bowling with.)

So there you have it – 20 things you can now say NO to and use what would've been a huge waste of your time in a much more productive way ... like sleeping!

Enjoy your new freedom.

-MJ Wilson

It All Depends On What You beLIEve

You don't have to fit into someone else's world to belong in your own

---

"What is *wrong* with you? Nobody else acts like this."

"We're so disappointed in you! How could you do this to us?"

"Why do you ALWAYS have to be so difficult? Can't you just fit in like everyone else?"

Sound familiar? How many times have people asked you one or more of those questions, over and over, throughout your entire life? And regardless of how often they ask, the questioning never seems to get any easier to hear.

Why?

Well, besides the fact that it's just plain annoying, those questions usually come from the people we care about the most: our family and friends. And although I'm sure they mean well … (okay … actually I *don't* know that – but for now let's hope for the best), I imagine you feel like they're asking you those questions because they don't want you to be happy or don't want you to succeed. And technically, I suppose this could be true. But honestly, I don't believe it's the real reason they're asking.

I'm willing to bet your "uniqueness" and free spirit make them a little uncomfortable – and not so much because you're so socially strange or morally wrong (although your family might disagree), but because you're showing them what's possible when people (like you!) truly follow their passion in life and are free to express themselves however they choose, regardless of what others may think.

YOU represent possibility.

Living your life "out-loud" may remind them of who they used to be or wish they were. I'm not saying they wish they were you. I'm just saying it's possible they wish they had the freedom you have – the freedom to be whatever it is you want to be, despite what your family, friends or culture say you *have* to be.

Every day that you're living free in front of them is a day they're reminded they aren't. And for some of them, that hurts.

So they decide to hurt you ...

"What gives you the right?"
"Who do you think you are?"
"Can't you see how much you're embarrassing us?"

And those are just the questions.

"You look ridiculous. You *can't* be serious."
"You need to seek help. You make no sense."
"You *have* to change or we're going to disown you."

If you must endure one or more of these questions or comments on a consistent basis, I feel for you. (*Really ... I do.* It's why I'm writing this story.) No one should have to put up with such undeserved pain or prejudice. And based on what I know, odds are, you've been mocked, bullied, discriminated against, abused and in some extreme cases, you may have even had your life threatened. But if this is true, please allow me to encourage you to not lose hope! I believe there are reasons for this (*not* excuses) and they may explain why your family and friends (or even your enemies) are doing this to you:

- **Ignorance** – They simply don't have any knowledge or understanding of what you're doing or why. This makes them uncomfortable and causes them to want YOU to change for THEIR comfort – something that is not only wrong, but also selfish.

- **Fear** – Due to stereotypes, they may have a negative misconception about what you believe or represent and therefore fear what you are or may become.

- **Hate** – The worst of the three, this trait is often empowered by an external source, typically utilizing ignorance *and* fear to create its "values."

I realize there may be other reasons, but these three are some of the most common. And as harsh as they are, there *are* some steps you can take to help reduce or even eliminate them (or their effects) in your life, if you're willing to put in some effort and practice a little bit of patience. For example:

- **Teaching and Understanding** – which helps eliminate ignorance

- **Showing and Giving Love** – which drives out fear

- **Instigating Legal Means** – which unfortunately, is sometimes the best defense against hate

But even if you do all of these, I don't believe your problem will be solved. Why? Because they don't address the main source of your problem.

I believe there's a deeper source. A source that feeds their growth, much like the root of a tree feeds its branches. A source that is often buried under layers of hurt and pain, cleverly disguised as "concern" or "care" for your own well-being.

Have you ever considered the idea that maybe the reason your family and friends (and even your enemies) are asking you those questions, making those comments, or treating you the way they are isn't because they don't want you to be happy or to succeed, but rather, because *they're* not happy and *they* haven't succeeded?

In other words, *maybe they're the problem, not you.*

You've heard the saying, "Misery loves company," right? Well if this is true, then failure certainly doesn't want to hang out with success. Which means those among your family and friends who have given up on their dreams don't want to hang out with people like you!

Now that's not a popular opinion, I know. But like I always say, "I didn't come here to fit in, I came here to tell the truth." So let me share a simple truth with you:

If two of you are the same, one of you is not necessary.

(Meditate on that for a moment before moving on to the next sentence, please.)

You don't have to believe what your family and friends want you to believe.

You don't have to do what they want you to do.

You don't even have be what they want you to be. (That statement alone should be enough to make you smile and press on!)

You were created with your own brain for a reason – and it wasn't so someone else's brain could control yours.

Relax.

Take a deep breath.

Exhale.

Sit quietly where you are.

And realize you ... YES YOU – the "oddball" of the family – you are special just as you are.

Just because you don't behave, believe, love, care, date, eat, dress, live, marry, talk, think, practice, pray, try, want or work like everyone else, it doesn't mean they're right and you're wrong. It just means you're *you*.

One of the reasons you *are* necessary is because you *are* different – so celebrate your uniqueness!

The world needs what you have to offer – art, acceptance, brains, beauty, skill, talent, bravery, hope, style, culture, diversity, fashion, music, character, personality, livelihood, proof, understanding, faith, and on and on ...

If you conform, we risk losing all of that – all that you could (and should) make available to us. What a tragedy it would be to have you here, on this planet, for such a time as this, and yet not share your gift!

It's *your time*.

Express yourself.

Speak up for those who can't.

And **show the world** how to live ... *free*.

-*MJ Wilson*

Repeat Offender

The problem isn't that they're not right for us. The problem is that it feels so good to be wrong with them

He doesn't care.
He never will.
And you know it. Yet you keep going back.
Why?

Does he deserve another chance? (You know he doesn't.)
Do you deserve so much better? (You know you do.)

So why do you keep going back?

It's so bad now that you actually have to hide what you're doing. If your family and friends knew, they'd scold you. Correct you. "Solve" you.

So you go ... silently and hopefully, you go.

And when you see him, your heart flutters. Your hopes awaken. Your fantasy becomes all the more real. Until it happens ...

He leaves you. Again.
And the pain starts all over. Again.
And the wound reopens. Again.
And you can't let it heal.

So why? Why do you go back, time and time again, knowing he's just going to do it to you again?

Because you're addicted, that's why.

And although it hurts like hell and you know it's never gonna work, for that brief moment when you see him, and the picture you've had in your mind of what was or possibly could be is now right in front of you, it seemingly makes all the pain bearable, if only for a minute, an hour, or if you're "lucky," a day.

I didn't write this to "fix" you, and I don't pretend to have all the answers. All I know is, when you're truly ready to get over him and move on to the love you deserve, the transformation will begin. The key is to know the difference between love and addiction.

Love replenishes, addiction depletes.

Stop listening to what he says, stop believing in what he's about, and start looking at what he does. Focus on what he's doing *to* you (or not doing *for* you) instead of rehearsing how he made you feel "that one time at that one place when he said or did that one thing."

Life is made up of billions and billions of moments in time. You are certainly worth more than one of them.

-MJ Wilson

Because I'm Your Daughter, *Not* Your _____!

That moment when you realize your parents treat you like everything they've ever wanted instead of what you actually are – their DAUGHTER!

Although several of the scenarios listed below could easily apply to a son, I wanted to give my female friends a chance to share their voice. Therefore, I decided to keep this story 100 percent female, asking only the ladies to fill in the blank to this story's title.

I put together a list of the top 10 best answers, along with the explanations that came with them, in an effort to shed some light on a problem I call "misplaced expectations."

Perhaps you – possibly the recipient of a jaded parent relationship – will see that it's not your fault for *not* being something you were never meant to be and don't have to be. You are free to be "you" and you only.

Meanwhile, if you're a parent: time to pay attention. Who knows? You may even start treating your daughter the way she's always deserved to be treated – as a beautiful creation *from* you, rather than an undeserving extension *of* you.

I'm hoping for the best.

-MJ Wilson

1) Because I'm your daughter, not your: BEST FRIEND!

Why does my mother feel the need to tell me she's having an affair behind my father's back? I DON'T WANT TO KNOW ABOUT THIS! It only puts me in an awkward position every time I see my dad. If I don't tell him, I feel like I'M the one who's betraying him. If I DO tell him, I feel like I'm betraying my mother's trust. It's not fair to put me in this position.

Cherelle 22 / Wichita, KS

2) Because I'm your daughter, not your: TROPHY!

No matter what I accomplish, my mother finds a way to spin it around and somehow take credit for it! When I posted a pic of me getting my degree, she wrote, "Look at that smart young lady *I* raised." (She took credit for my hard work, rather than posting something like, "I'm so proud of you" or "I knew you could do it!")

When we're at church and someone compliments me on my hair, she'll interrupt and say, "Well ... I wonder who taught her how to do it like *that*." (As if EVERY hairstyle I have comes from her.)

If I decorate my home, improve my yard, lose weight, cook a meal or even change my nail polish, somehow ... some way, she manages to let EVERYONE know, "That's my daughter and I taught her *everything* she knows."

Mariah 38 / Boise, ID

3) Because I'm your daughter, not your: SUBSTITUTE!

Coming from a family of seven and being the eldest child (I have three brothers and one sister), when I was growing up I ALWAYS had to play the role of an extra parent. You wouldn't believe how many times I had to change my brothers' and sister's diapers, clean up their messes, babysit on the weekends, do their laundry, help with their homework, fix their dinner *and* do their dishes! I was never allowed to be their older sister. Instead I became their "third parent." It got so bad at one time that they actually started calling me "Mom."

Jane 53 / Salt Lake City, UT

4) Because I'm your daughter, not your: <u>PERSONAL BANKER</u>!

My father drinks and gambles his paycheck away week after week while my mother blows her check on a new pair of shoes or the latest fashion accessory. The next thing you know, they can't afford to pay their rent, buy groceries or put gas in their cars and then somehow come to the conclusion that because I have a good job and a little bit of savings that I should be the one to bail them out.

It wouldn't be so bad if this happened once or twice on occasion, but this has been going on all my life.

It's not a problem, *it's a pattern*.

Adya 41 / Sioux Falls, SD

5) Because I'm your daughter, not your: <u>BARBIE DOLL</u>!

Apparently my mother thinks I'm her Barbie Doll because she continually tells me where I'm going to go to college, what my career is going to be, who I'm going to marry and how many children I'm going to have. (She's even gone so far as to tell me what names she'll "allow" me to choose when naming my future children!) It's like I'm not allowed to think for myself.

She doesn't trust me to make good decisions, yet she's the one who raised me.

Mia 17 / Honolulu, HI

6) Because I'm your daughter, not your: <u>SON</u>!

My problem has always been more with my father than my mother. Apparently I'm the "son he never had." (He even named me "Bobbi" instead of "Bobby" just so he could have his name carried on.) When I was a little girl I wanted to take ballerina lessons. He refused, telling me "Dancing is for sissies" and then signed me up for karate lessons. A few years later when I wanted to try out for the cheerleading squad, again, he said no, and this time he signed me up for basketball. When I graduated from high school and left for college, I wanted to be a schoolteacher and teach preschool. *He* wanted me to be a doctor and take over his practice.

Until now I never realized … all these years I've been working to be the son he never had instead of the woman I've always wanted to be.

Dr. Bobbi 56 / Burlington, VT

7) Because I'm your daughter, not your: <u>THERAPIST</u>!

My mother can never just call or stop by to say hello or to see how *I'm* doing. It seems she always has some hidden agenda buried in a "victim mentality" that usually includes her unloading all her problems on me. She typically goes on and on about how miserable she is in her marriage or how much she hates her job (even though she refuses to do anything about either of them). Today she told me she feels like a total failure in life and often wishes she had never been born.

Can somebody *please* tell me … What am *I* supposed to do with this information?

Crystal 33 / Cheyenne, WY

8) Because I'm your daughter, not your: SECOND CHANCE!

My mother got pregnant at 17 and had to give up her scholarship to college. Of course, being the control freak that she is, she automatically assumed I'd follow in her footsteps and get pregnant during my teenage years, too. Swearing up and down "You'll never make the mistakes I made. I won't let you," she decided to *never* let me date a boy – EVER! I couldn't go to school dances, my friends' parties, or even stay over at my girlfriend's house. My senior year I *finally* convinced her to let me go to a dance – my prom – but even then I wasn't allowed to take a date. (She made my father drop me off at 8 and pick me up at 10. Who does that???)

I am now 21 years old and to this day *I've still never been on a date*. Now I know what you're thinking … "You're a grown woman now, Tanisha. You can do whatever you want." And I suppose you're right. But I'm also a grown woman attending a local community college (I'm currently a junior), so I still live at home with my parents. Going out on a date or bringing one home isn't exactly easy – my mother would freak out.

Sad thing is, even if I did go on a date, I wouldn't have a clue what to do. Neither of my parents taught me anything about dating (or sex, or love, or marriage).

I feel so behind and naïve. How am I ever going to learn from my mistakes if I'm never allowed to make them?

Tanisha 21 / Boston, MA

9) Because I'm your daughter, not your: SERVANT!

When I was a little girl, my stepfather always treated me like his personal servant. Now I'm not talking about the occasional, "Sweetie … do Daddy a favor and go get me another drink, please." Or even the more direct, "Lauren – take my plate into the kitchen and fix me some more food. NOW." No … that would be way too nice and possibly even reasonable. My stepdad was far worse. He would literally make me sit on the floor next to him in his reclining chair like some kind of dog on a leash. And then whenever he decided he wanted or needed something, he would bark out orders to me, while constantly telling my mother and me that we were useless pieces of trash that no man would ever want – always reminding us we could never make it without him.

This went on for years, nearly brainwashing us into believing we were worthless women, put on this planet simply to serve him. But one day, my 15th birthday to be exact, he went too far and said something I'll never forget:

"Birthday present? Are you serious Lauren? You think you deserve a birthday present? You're lucky to even be here in *my home*. I wanted to get rid of you the day I met your mother, but she convinced me to keep you around. Me allowing you to stay *is* your birthday present."

Something in me just snapped when he said that and I vowed I'd never get him another damn thing in my life. I packed my things that night and left, while he slept, passed out on the couch.

Ten years later and I'm doing just fine, thank you. I didn't need his abusive or evil ways then, and I don't need them now.

As for my mother, she's doing just fine, too. Who do you think drove the car the night I left?

Lauren 25 / Portland, ME

10) Because I'm your daughter, not your: <u>SPOUSE</u>!

For some reason my parents both expect me to do things for them that they should be doing for each other. For example, when my mother's high school reunion rolls around every five years, who do you think she asks to go with her? ME! And when she had her out-patient surgery last year and had to be driven two hours ONE WAY to the clinic, as well as have someone wait while she had the surgery (another two hours) and then drive her back home, who do you think she asked?

My dad's the same. When he was recognized for salesman of the year at his job and was honored at his company's annual banquet, who do you think he asked to go as his date? Or when he decided to take a weekend ski trip, guess who he asked to go with him? Or maybe I should say, guess who he DIDN'T ask to go with him? (He actually told me "Your mother always complains about the cold and never skis. She'll just get on my nerves.")

Uh ... What?

My parents don't like each other ... that's pretty obvious. They've basically been roommates their entire marriage. (They don't even sleep in the same bedroom and haven't for over a decade.) But rather than deal with the issues that have come between them over the years, they'd rather place the demand upon ME to fulfill the role of the spouse they never had.

Believe me, I don't mind being a good daughter and spending time with either of them. And I don't mind helping here and there, within reason – that's what family is for. But their lack of love for each other doesn't constitute the whoring-out of my love for them.

Amy 44 / Billings, MT

Staff Meetings ... Oh How I *HATE* Thee

Lack of participation doesn't necessarily mean an unwillingness to participate. It may just mean there's nothing worth participating in

"That was a one-hour, total-waste-of-my-time staff meeting that could've easily been done in a five-minute email."

How many times have we all said that? And yet, somehow, somewhere, the evil staff meeting-makers continue to crank out week after week, month after month, year after year, the most mundane, worthless, paper-wasting, time-consuming, pointless and repetitive agenda-making, dumbass joke-telling meetings we've ever endured. From the stupid "Let's get to know each other" co-worker game-filling meetings, to the annoying "I'm the boss so I need to hear myself speak" meetings, I think we can all agree, something has *got* to change.

And yet, we keep having them. Why?

Why do we continue to produce such never-ending nonsense when there are so many other things (productive *and* useful) that we could be doing with this time? (And I don't mean personally either – I mean things that could improve our place of work.) Yet, like cattle to the slaughterhouse, we move on in the same direction, day after day, year after year ... except unlike cattle, we know exactly where we're going. Which makes us even worse.

41

HEY! (Snapping my fingers twice and in your face!) Here's a quick thought: How about we save staff meetings for actual times when the staff needs to meet?

Do you have any idea how much time, employee power and money this could save? Here we are (the employees), sitting in excruciating meetings, repeating paragraphs and emails like talking parrots, falling asleep or daydreaming most of the time, just to accomplish what could've been accomplished in an email that took only minutes to create! Not only would this save time and money, but paper and resources, too!

Am I the only one who feels this way???

I once asked my boss at the end of one of our many staff meetings why he didn't just put it in an email. His reply?

"Because you all don't read your emails."

To which I replied, "Then how did we all know we were having a staff meeting today?"

(If looks could kill – or at least get you fired – I would've been dead/unemployed right there.)

Now, just so you know, contrary to my earlier rant, I am NOT against having staff meetings. **I'm against having staff meetings that are a waste of everyone's time!**

BIG DIFFERENCE.

Keeping that in mind, you may be wondering, "Well if that's true, when *should* we have a staff meeting? When are they appropriate?"

I'm so glad you asked. (Smile.)

I created the following guidelines to help you know when you should and should NOT have a staff meeting. (You can thank me later.)

EMPLOYERS: You should NOT have a staff meeting if ...

1. Whatever you're discussing can be done through an email. Have I said this already? Good. Read it again. (And again. And ...)

2. The day you scheduled it is the day you want to have it. (No surprise meetings! It's not fair to your employees or their time.)

3. It pertains only to a small sect of your employees and not your entire staff. (Ex: Just because Rick doesn't work well with Cameron, it doesn't mean no one else does, so everyone else doesn't need to hear about it! Deal with Rick and Cameron privately.)

4. You're doing it for any of the following reasons:

    - to hear yourself speak

    - to brag about your grandchildren

    - to share your favorite new joke or YouTube video

    - to feed your need to control your employees because you can't control your spouse or kids – ouch!

    - to spend quality time with those who work for you because you have no one at home to spend quality time with you (Sorry, but it's true.)

    - because you want everyone to see your new outfit (Yes, it happens.)

    - because you're so unorganized that you have "effed-up" everything at your place of business and now you need an emergency meeting so everyone else can bail you out. (C'mon! ... lead by example or get out of the way!)

EMPLOYERS: **You SHOULD have a staff meeting if …**

1. There is absolutely no way the topic can be dealt with successfully without everyone meeting in person.

2. See reason number 1 above.

On behalf of all employees around the world, and especially for those who cannot speak up for fear of being fired or demoted, let me just say …

We are tired, over-worked, underpaid, literate (meaning we *can* read emails!) adults (not kids, so stop treating us like your children), and we are professionals. We DO know what we're doing and we ARE capable of doing it.

To you, the employers, we want you to know, if we seem apathetic or uninvolved, it's not necessarily because we don't want to help or participate. It may just be because we feel there's nothing worth participating in! (Do we really need *another* committee? Seriously? UGH!)

So please … value our time and give us the respect we deserve and we'll give you the production you desire and the results you need.

And don't even think about saying, "Respect must be earned," because if that's true, then try earning ours first. You're supposed to be our *leader*, not our boss.

Signed,

Every employee on the planet

-MJ Wilson

YES, *I Had An Affair* ... And Your Point Is?

Don't spend all of your time stuck in one moment that was merely just one moment in time

An affair is an affair whether for a "good" reason (if you believe that's even possible) or a bad one. And although I believe I had a good reason for my affair, my goal is not to convince you of such. (And please note, I said reason, not *excuse*.) What I really want to do, and the goal of this letter, is to focus on a much bigger problem: why YOU are stuck on the fact that I had an affair, and why you can't seem to just let it go.

Now when I say "you," I mean *you*: my family, my friends, my colleagues, my neighbors and even my church. Why can't you just let it go? It's been more than three years now and you still won't drop it.

What does it take? What do you want from me? An apology? A confession? Should I go into hiding? Move to another town? Become a recluse? What is it that you expect from me?

Some say maybe I should explain how it happened and why. Perhaps that would help. But would it? I mean, think about it, I could easily rant on and on about how my affair was a lapse of judgment on my part or a flaw in my character – how, although this was one moment in my life (I do own up to it), it shouldn't be *the* defining moment of my life. I mean, I have gone on to do other things you know, some of them being rather great achievements – like getting my PhD after my 42nd birthday, or as a single parent and mother now, how I'm raising my daughter (the best thing that ever came out of that affair) to be so much more than I ever dreamed or imagined. Yes, I could do that.

Or I could easily share with you how I was physically and emotionally abused by my husband. How he treated me like a sex object for his personal use, put on this Earth to bring him pleasure with no regard for my own self-worth or feelings. Or how he would often tell me, "You're to be seen, not heard" and then slap me around when his anger got the best of him if I had an opinion that disagreed with his. What if I told you that? What if I told you this went on for years and years and no one ever knew because I protected him and his reputation so as not to defame our name or his position in the church? Would I at least have your sympathy and prayers if not your forgiveness?

You see, I could do that. All of that. I could explain, apologize, and ask for your forgiveness. But should I? Do I really owe *you* an explanation or an apology? Do I really need *your* forgiveness?

The point I'm trying to make is, regardless of what I did, that's just it … I did it. Not you. *I've dealt with it and moved on and you should, too.* To continue to bring up my past is a blatant attempt to keep me from ever succeeding in my future. It's like watching me slip and fall on a banana peel and then immediately picking it up and throwing it back in front of me hoping I'll slip on it again.

Not only is it wrong, *it's just plain evil.*

Listen … Everyone (and I do mean *everyone*) has dealt with or is currently dealing with something. Whether it be an affair, divorce, addiction, unplanned pregnancy, depression, family quarrel, unhappy marriage, financial blunder, flunking out, lying, cheating, stealing, failing, quitting, starting, hurting, and on and on and on. We all have our problems and vices. *All of us.* But if there's one thing I've learned through all of this, it's this: "Placing the blame is pointless, but owning the problem is priceless."

So why don't we start there? Let's stop blaming everyone and everything else for our poor choices and failures in life. Let's own up to them, deal with them and move on.

I did.

I stopped blaming my ex-husband for my affair. I stopped blaming my lover for my affair. I stopped blaming God, my family, my friends, my life, my circumstances, my depression and anything else I could think of. Not because it's not their fault or because it's all mine, but because it doesn't matter. What matters is owning the problem. If I own it then it's mine. If it's mine then I can do with it what I like.

I've "owned" this affair – I admitted I did it. I've dealt with it accordingly – based on my beliefs and standards, *not yours*. And I've chosen to leave it behind. I refuse to allow something from my past to dictate my future.

So, having said all that, for those of you in my life who can't seem to grasp this concept and how it works, please … feel free to continue harassing me, judging me and reminding me daily of my so-called shortcomings (according to you and your standards).

Really. Go for it. I wouldn't blame you if you did. And I won't.

I'll just own you next – like I do all my problems.

And then I'll leave your ass behind … just like I left his.

-Kimberly / Tulsa, OK

Don't Make Me Slap You

Sometimes the amount of energy required to preserve something is greater than the amount of good it provides for keeping it

The following Q&A sessions are problems I hear all too often. Perhaps listing them here, along with my advice, will help some of you alleviate your pain ... or at least wake you up.

THE OTHER WOMAN
Dear MJ: As soon as he saves up enough money, he's gonna leave her. He promised me. Besides, their marriage is practically over anyway. I've waited three years, what's one or two more?

-Melissa / Phoenix, AZ

REALITY CHECK: What's one or two more? Are you kidding me? That's an extra 17,520 hours of your life you'll NEVER get back! That's what it is! And that's if, and ONLY if he ACTUALLY leaves her! The fact that he's been with both of you for three years now is proof to him he *can* have the best of both worlds *without* leaving! And let me guess, she doesn't know about you, but you know all about her, right? Therefore, YOU have to live your life around her and always be "on call" or "Plan B." In other words, you are SECOND. Do you see this? And please don't tell me, "Oh but you don't understand ... when he's with me the love we make is amazing!" Really? Well how do you think he got so good at it?

Remember this, whatever he's doing with you, he's already done with her – and may be doing with someone else while he's seeing you!

As the old saying goes, "Why buy the cow when the milk is free?" Honey, you're getting milked! Please, do yourself a favor and walk away. Don't waste another precious minute of your beautiful life and amazing love on someone who doesn't deserve it or preserve it. You CAN move on, you CAN find someone who puts you first and you CAN be truly happy. Believe me, people do it every day. But one thing I know for sure, *you CAN'T grab a hold of your future success if you're still holding onto your past failures.*

Let it (and him) go.

THE "YOU-REALLY-NEED-TO-GET-A-CLUE" EX-BOYFRIEND

Dear MJ: How long should I chase my ex-girlfriend? I've been trying to get back with her for a year and a half now. I believe she truly loved me before, so I believe she can (and will) truly love me again. I'm hoping she'll leave the guy she's with now (he's no good for her anyway) and come back eventually, but I'm getting tired of waiting. What should I do?

-Cody / Concord, NH

REALITY CHECK: Did you just say "chase her?" Are you serious? You're chasing her??? Oh wow … let me help you. This isn't 5th grade … you're not playing a game of Tag on the playground. You don't chase women, you *pursue* them. If you're chasing her, that means she's running from you. If she's running from you, it means she doesn't wanna be caught by you.

Stop chasing her and find a new woman worthy of your pursuit.

Never beg for that which you have the ability to acquire without doing so. Besides, begging doesn't make you look weak, it proves that you *are* weak.

P.S. Leave the other guy out of it. If he's that bad and she chose him, what's that say about her? (And she chose you at one point, so what's that say about her perception of you?)

THE "MO' MONEY, MO' PROBLEMS" ENTREPRENEUR

Dear MJ: They said this year is THE year for sales to blow up! I'm so excited! No more 9-5. No more 40-hour work week. I'm about to be financially free! All I have to do is pay an initial fee of $400 to sign up and then agree to buy at least $200 worth of our company's product each month. Then I need to hold at least two one-hour meetings per week in my home (or my friends' homes) explaining to them and others why they need to join as well. I also have to sign up at least two of them and convince them to do the same thing (so I qualify to be paid).

And speaking of being paid, there's always room to grow! If I sign up to purchase $400 worth of products per month instead, I qualify for even more weekly pay! And, what's more, they're constantly offering training seminars!

For only $800 (+ airfare and hotel expenses) I can go to this year's conference in VEGAS (Yessss!) and learn how to make money from the MOST SUCCESSFUL PEOPLE IN THE BUSINESS! (Where else can you get access to this type of information??? These people are so rich they don't even need the money!) And the trainings they offer have all kinds of sales tools and kits to help me improve my business! (If I pay an additional $75 I can get free access to the entire conference digitally, VIP access to all the speakers one hour before the seminar PLUS my own virtual office online for one full year!!! It's like owning my own business!)

It's such an amazing company! Yet when I talk to my family and friends about it none of them seem interested. They never return my calls. They never reply to my emails. And they always cancel our meetings at the last minute. It's like they're avoiding me.

I don't get it. This is such a great way to make money.

Am I missing something here?

-Jeremy / Richmond, VA

REALITY CHECK: Ummm … (Insert a brief video here of me staring blankly into the camera with a very confused, somewhat hopeless look on my face. I then let out a long sigh, shake my head back and forth, and order a strong drink.) *Jeremy, Jeremy, Jeremy* … There are so many things I could say here, but I'm not here to "win" an argument, I'm here to make you think. Therefore, I'll keep this simple.

WHO WAS YOUR MATH TEACHER???

Listen to me … There are a zillion of these types of businesses. Some have a great product, but a horrible payout. (Easy to sell, but you rarely make any money.) Others have a worthless product with a great payout. (Hard to sell, so you rarely see big money.) And to be fair, there are a few that have a great product *and* a great payout. (Notice I said "few.") In your case, regardless of the product or payout, it sounds like you have found one that requires more money FROM you than it's giving TO you. And trust me, that is more than enough to scare away your family and friends.

You asked "Am I missing something here?" and I believe you are, but I think I have an idea that should help. Try this: Keep a running total of every dollar you spend on a monthly basis just to be a part of this company (gas money, products, brochures, trips, commission fees, etc.) and compare it to the amount of money you actually make (after taxes) from this company in the same amount of time. I think you'll see what I mean.

If that doesn't work, go find an elementary math class and have a seat.

THE PAINFULLY PROTECTIVE PARENTS
Dear MJ: We hate to admit it, but you were right … Our son did ask to move back in with us again (Yes … for the third time.) And we know we told you we weren't going to allow it, BUT, we are his parents, and we just hate the thought of not being there for our baby when he needs us most.

Although we just love having David back in our home, he's only been back two months and we're already experiencing difficulty.

Gary paid his car payment last month and this month (since David's separation, he has practically no money) and of course he pays no rent or utilities here (we could never ask him to do that). We've tried to ease his pain as much as possible during this difficult time by taking care of the little things in his life (I do his laundry, fix his food, etc.) but to be honest, all of this is taking a toll on us as well ... financially and emotionally – especially since she isn't doing anything to help!

We think we should talk to her and ask her to do her part ... Problems or not, she is STILL a part of his life! However, we don't want to be viewed as weak/bad parents by reaching out to her – we just couldn't live with ourselves if David thought we weren't able to provide for him, especially now.

What do you think we should do?

-Linda & Gary / Providence, RI

REALITY CHECK: Difficult time? Really? Please explain to me how your 38 year-old "baby" living in his parents' basement, paying no rent or utilities, having his meals and laundry done by his mother and his car payment paid by his father, could possibly be going through a "difficult time" right now. Those problems you are attempting to solve for him are the very problems he needs to solve on his own so he will think twice before repeating this process again. (Or should I say "For the THIRD time"?)

And while I'm at it, to whom are you referring when you say "she?" His first wife? Or the one he's cheating on now? (Did you forget you told me about that previously?) Besides these women all being used and misled, what about his daughter from the first marriage who doesn't understand why her daddy left one day for someone else?

I know all this sounds harsh, but it brings to mind an old saying I read years ago: "A wound from a friend is better than a kiss from the enemy." I have to agree. Sometimes the truth *is* hard to swallow, but it *will* set you free if you're bold enough to look it square in the eyes and see it for what it really is. And I think that's exactly what you need to do – get honest with yourself and with him. It's time for him to grow up and become the husband and father he should be, not the single man or baby that he wants to be.

If that's not convincing enough for you, look at it this way: How would you like it if your son treated *you* the way he's treated these women? What if he used *you* for money, a place to live, companionship, cooking, cleaning, free meals and financial help, only to prepare himself to leave you with no warning whatsoever, in the near future, whenever he felt like it?

Oh wait … my bad. *He already is.*

- MJ Wilson

You're Not Blind.
You Just Can't See

Just because you haven't won, doesn't mean you've lost. It might just mean you haven't finished

Okay, so things didn't quite turn out the way you planned.

You thought you'd be finished with your schooling by now.

You thought you'd be working your dream job by now.

You thought you'd be further along with everything by now.

Instead, you've got a baby you didn't plan for, a job you hate, and your bills seem higher than your income.

What's worse, they told you that you wouldn't make it. They said your dream was too big. And now it seems they were right.

You feel hopeless and embarrassed.

BUT I SAY look at you ... your character traits, your abilities, your talent. If anyone could make it happen, especially now, it's YOU.

Yes, you have that baby. But that baby has never missed a meal, never been neglected and never felt anything but your love. This shows your tenacity, perseverance and ability to deal with the unexpected.

54

Yes, you hate your job. But you do it well and people like you there. This shows your work ethic, your ability to control your emotions and your capacity to shine even in unhappy conditions.

Yes, you have bills (and bills, and bills), but somehow you manage to pay your rent each month, put food on your table and still buy your baby new clothes. Although I'm sure you feel financially stretched, all of this shows your ability to get a lot out of little, make the most of what you've got and prioritize your needs above your wants.

You say you failed. *But I say you haven't finished.*

(Since when did we start having time limits on our dreams?)

So I ask you, when they said you would never make it, why do you still believe them? With all these characteristics, I think it's easy to see, if ANYONE could find a way to turn things around, it's YOU.

I just wish you could see it, too.

-MJ Wilson

Don't Get It Twisted

*Some people punish their present potential
with their past pain*

So there I was the day before the big day – Valentine's Day – looking for a bra and panties for my girl Britney. We had been together for nearly three months, and although we hadn't had sex (yet), I wanted to get her something intimate and personal to show her how much I cared about her. Something … *from my heart.*

After roaming around the store a few minutes, and feeling a little embarrassed as a 25-year-old guy in this kind of store, I finally decided to just go to the counter and ask for help. Five minutes later, I was on my way to my car with a very sexy outfit (along with a matching robe and slippers), highly recommended by not one, but two of the women working in the store. One of them actually said, "Trust us … She's gonna love this." So I did. I threw in a box of chocolates and some flowers and everything was cool.

The next day I arrived at Britney's house around 7 o'clock. I had on my best cologne, favorite t-shirt and jeans, and of course, my new Jordans. I looked good, smelled good and felt great. I just knew it was gonna be a great night and I couldn't wait to give Britney her gifts.

As soon as I walked in I placed her flowers and chocolates in the fridge and her main gifts on the coffee table. I told her she had to promise me she wouldn't look, but it didn't matter … she wasn't paying me much attention anyway. She was still in her old clothes (sweats and t-shirt) and consumed with cooking our dinner.

Speaking to me like she hadn't heard a thing I'd said so far, she then told me that I had "better like this meal" because she wasn't going to make it again anytime soon.

"I know, Baby," I told her. "I got you. You know I love all that you do for me."

(Now I realize her welcome wasn't exactly the best a guy can get, but I just let it slide. I was in a good mood, it was Valentine's Day and the food smelled great. Why argue now?)

After we finished eating, I told her, "I'll clean up the dishes so you can take a break. All I want you to do is sit on the couch and relax. As soon as I'm done, we can give each other our Valentine's gifts."

Big mistake.

"Gifts?" she snapped. "*What* gifts? You just *got* your gift! What … a meal that took me THREE HOURS to make not good enough for you?"

She then shook her head and sat down on the couch, mumbling something about people not appreciating anything she does. I didn't know why she was upset, and I didn't wanna ask. Again, I just let it slide. Not because it didn't bother me, but because I felt bad for Britney. She was a wonderful girl who seemingly had a streak of bad luck with the wrong guys. I wanted to change that. I wanted her to see that I was different and not like the others.

I wanted her to see that I cared.

I apologized for the misunderstanding, told her I LOVED the meal (and I did), thanked her for all her hard work, and then went to the kitchen to get her flowers and chocolates. I thought for sure they would make her feel better and I also believed it would show her that somebody *did* appreciate her – ME!

Big mistake.

As I handed them to her she said "thanks" but didn't seem too impressed. Next, she opened the robe and slippers. Same result – not too interested. I didn't care. I was so excited – I just knew she was gonna love the next gift I got her and couldn't wait for her to see what it was.

As she untied the ribbon and pulled back the wrapping, she let out a deep sigh, looked me straight in the eyes and said something I will never, ever forget:

"What the hell is this? You think I'm some kinda *hoe* or something? Like you can just buy your way into my pants? Do I look like a piece of meat to you?"

I just sat there in shock. Where was all this coming from? What did I do to deserve this? What she said ticked me off, but more than anything else, it hurt my feelings. I put a lot of thought and effort into her gift but she didn't care.

"I'm in there, workin' my ass off for three hours makin' you the best damn meal of your life, and all you can think about is getting me in bed??? Unbelievable!"

She threw her gift across the room and stood up. "You're just like all the rest! All you want is sex! God forbid you get something for ME, Brandon! Something … *from your heart*!"

And with that, she stormed into her bedroom and slammed the door. I tried to explain but she wouldn't let me in and she wouldn't listen. She told me to get the hell out and never come back.

So I did.

For her to compare me to all those jerks from her past wasn't fair. I didn't deserve their punishment and she didn't deserve my love. It was a sad, pathetic ending to what should have been a great day. And unfortunately, it was the end of us.

Now don't get me wrong, I actually did try to work things out. But she wouldn't answer my calls or return my texts. And I wasn't about to just drive over there and beg for her to let me into her home (or heart) at the door. I cared about her, yes. But I cared about myself, too. So, I moved on.

Since dating Britney, I've come to realize that what happened between us wasn't really about me doing anything wrong, but about Britney not accepting anything right. She had issues far beyond anything my gifts that night could fix. And what's worse, she gave up the chance to be with someone like me who was willing to work through all those issues with her.

You see, what she doesn't know, and what I never told her (because she wouldn't let me explain) was that I was adopted at the age of six, one week before Valentine's Day. And one of the earliest memories I have of my parents is the day – Valentine's Day – my father gave my mother flowers, a box of chocolates and a fancy, ribbon-wrapped gift (much like the one I had given Britney). I remember how excited and happy my mother was to get them.

At the time, I had no idea what my father had gotten my mother (I *was* only six), but later learned it was a robe, slippers and yes … lingerie.

To this day my mother still speaks of *that* day – Valentine's Day – whenever she reminisces about my father. It's one of her favorite memories of him. And because I looked up to my father the way I did, I think you can see where my heart was when I bought Britney her gift.

As for Britney … I had no intention of having sex with her that night. She told me when we first met that she was tired of guys only wanting her for her body, and that I would "have to wait until the time was right." I respected her for that and told her it was fine with me.

I thought she seemed a bit difficult at first, but I figured she'd see how much I care and eventually relax a little. The fact that I was there three months later on Valentine's Day and we still hadn't had sex should've been proof enough. I was fine with no sex. All I wanted was for her to like me the way my mother liked my father. And *that's* why I gave her the gifts.

With the history we now had between us, and the way that our relationship ended, I figured I'd never speak to Britney again. However, two years later I was at a shoe store in the mall when she walked in. She saw me and started coming my way. I hadn't seen her since we broke up, so I tried to play it off, but she just kept coming. I remember thinking to myself, "Well, this oughta be interesting." As she approached, she rattled off something about me looking good and then said, "How you been, boo? Long time, no see."

Big mistake.

I should mention Tiffany, my new girlfriend and fiancée, was sitting on a bench a few feet away trying on a pair of shoes. When she heard what Britney said to me, she immediately walked over and stood right behind her.

"Boo? Girl I don't know who you talkin' to, but the only boo around here is Brandon – and *he's mine.*"

Ooooooh! You should've seen the look on Britney's face! When she turned around and saw Tiffany, she was embarrassed, astonished *and* speechless. It was priceless.

Tiffany then immediately (and purposely) reached her hand out to mine, her engagement ring glaring in the light, and gave me a quick kiss. She then looked directly at Britney while speaking to me and said, "You ready ... *BOO?*"

Britney, still embarrassed and little upset, decided to take one last stab at the conversation before we could leave.

"Oh, I'm sorry Brandon," she said. "Is this your new piece of meat?"

Big mistake.

Tiffany, *not me*, without missing a beat, replied instantly.

"Piece of meat? Oh no baby. *Don't get it twisted.*" (As she waves her ring finger and shakes her head.) "I'm not his piece of meat. I'm his fiancée – **I'm the whole damn meal.**"

We were married two months later. And Valentine's Day is now my favorite holiday – *again*.

-Brandon / Trenton, NJ

The Father Who Never Was

A sacrifice should not be judged or valued based upon the benefit it gives its recipient, but rather, upon the detriment it causes the one sacrificing

I, Jason, am a happily married man and father of two. My wife, Sarah, is the most beautiful woman on Earth and the most loving mother I know. She and I both love our children – Jacob, 10, and Madison, 9 – more than life itself, and we pride ourselves on being "The best parents possible at all times."

Before we ever decided to have children, we vowed to do two things: give them a better life than we had; and love them better than our parents loved us. (Especially *my* parents.) And I must say, until last week, after only 11 years of marriage, I thought we had easily accomplished both. By all accounts, it seemed we had done far more for our kids than either of our parents had ever done for us. In our minds we were in a league of our own. But after a few drinks, one comment and a long conversation with my father, all that changed.

It was my father's 61st birthday and although I am one of three children, I, along with my wife and kids, was the only sibling to make the two-hour drive for my father's celebration. My mother had made his favorite dinner and dessert (Fettuccine Alfredo and German chocolate cake) and after stuffing ourselves full of both, my father and I retired to his "Man Cave" for a drink while the ladies cleaned up and the kids played. Typically this would be the time where my father, a high school dropout who made a lifelong career as a door-to-door salesman, would have a few too many drinks, and on rare occasion, talk to me more like his son and less like a customer. Normally I enjoyed these talks. They usually consisted of the "I'm proud of the man you've become" type of stuff and made me feel appreciated.

As I stoked the fireplace located just beneath an ugly picture of myself from my senior year in high school, my father pours us another drink. (I think to him, we weren't completely enjoying the Man Cave until we had a few drinks of our own not available to the women.) He then began his typical, but heartfelt speech.

"You've certainly made me proud, son," he said. "With your college degree and job promotions ... you've really grown into the man I always knew you could be ... one that loves and cares for his children very much. I know you'll always be there for them, the way your mother and I are always there for you."

Now I'm sure that sounds great to you, but what you don't understand is, although my father says he loves me very much and is very proud of who I've become, he *never* showed it growing up.

He was never there for me ...

Not at my games, my practices, or even just to pass ball in the backyard. Other than the occasional last minute appearance at a tournament or awards banquet, I honestly can't remember anything he attended at all. He was either always at work or too tired to play.

It hurt a lot growing up, and hurts me even more now ... especially being a parent myself.

As he hands me my drink (my first from him, my third for the night), I take a seat in one of two huge, leather-bound chairs while he stands near the mantle, continuing to boast. "When I look at you," he stated, "I see how much you love Jacob and Madison ... how well you treat them. How you'd do anything for them. You remind me of ME ... a chip of the ole block. You love your kids they the way your mother and I loved, and still love, you and your sisters. And I think it's great."

I don't know if it was my pride that got in the way, or the best of the whiskey from my last drink that was doing all the talking, but for some reason *I just couldn't let this slide*. Not this time. Not this year. I had worked too hard to become the father I am to just sit back and let him take all the credit for it. I had heard this speech a million times before and said nothing about it, but this time was different. Something in me snapped. And I went off …

"Chip off the ole block? Are you crazy? How am I ANYthing like you?

I pass football with Jacob *all the time*.

I practice soccer with Madison *all the time*.

I go to *all* their games and *all* their practices. Every play, every recital.

I've never missed an awards banquet or school presentation! NOT ONE!

Hell, I even play in the snow, run through the sprinkler, and go to the pool with them!

When did you EVER do that for me? For any of us kids for that matter? You were never there … *never*."

No sooner did that last statement fly out of my mouth before my father shot a glare at me like never before. I went from a man on a mission to a dwarfed little boy in about two seconds. "What was I thinking?" I thought to myself. "Why did I just say that?" I could tell I had hurt my father deeply and began to prepare for the worst.

"You're right," he said, as he walks over to me. "I never was there for you. Yes Jason, you are exactly right. But what you have failed to realize is *why* I was never 'there' for you. So let me help you …

You and your sisters were allowed to play as many sports as you wanted – baseball, cheerleading, basketball, volleyball, football, cross country, track, summer soccer teams … hell you even tried tennis one year and quit after only four practices! How do you think you and your sisters were able to play all those sports?

WHERE DO YOU THINK THE MONEY CAME FROM?

They weren't free you know. The cleats, the racquets, the gloves, uniforms, gas money, the basketball shoes you just 'had to have,' practice jerseys, participation fees, summer camp tuition and on and ON AND ON!!!

WHO DO YOU THINK PAID FOR ALL OF THAT?

That was ME! – your dad who was *'never there.'*

I worked 50-60 hours a week your entire childhood, just so your mother and I could afford to give you and your sisters the opportunities neither of us had – EVER!"

His bottom lip began to quiver.

"What you don't know, 'boy,' is that your mother and I took a vow long before you and your sisters were ever born … A vow that when we have children, we would accomplish two things above all else: give them a better life than we had; and love them better than our parents loved us. And considering my father walked out on me when I was four and we were too poor to ever play ANY organized sports, own a ball or even buy a uniform – I think I did a DAMN GOOD JOB of keeping my vow!

So you're right … I never was *there* for you. But it wasn't because I didn't want to be or because I didn't care … it was because I was working hard so that YOU could be there yourself."

Total silence for the next 20 seconds.

What do you say to that? I sank further into my chair, my head dropping to my chest, my heart beating heavy. What the hell is wrong with me? What was I thinking? I'd been so blind all these years … so busy striving to become "The best parent possible" that I had failed to see I had become one of the most ungrateful sons imaginable.

As my father stood there, his glass trembling in his hand and one tear streaming down his face, I slowly stood up, ashamedly walked over to him, put my hand on his shoulder, and said the first thing that came to my mind … the one thing I had never said to him in all 35 years of my life …

"Thank you Dad … *Thank you.*"

And then I hugged him like the little boy that I was so many years ago. I didn't want to let go. I began to cry. I apologized and told him how sorry I was for what I had said.

It felt like I had a new father, but in reality, he had a new son. It was surreal.

Ever since that day, Sarah and I have kept good on our vows to our children. We still believe we are some of "The best parents possible" and strive to be at all times. But along with our vows, and in light of this new awareness, we both decided to add one more vow to our list, and possibly the most important vow of all: To be "The most thankful children we can be" – especially while we still have our parents around to be thankful for.

-Jason / Hartford, CT

You Can't Handle The Truth!

Some people want honesty,
but most just want their back scratched

Col. Jessup: I'll answer the question. You want answers?
Lt. Kaffee: I think I'm entitled!
Col. Jessup: You want answers?!
Lt. Kaffee: I want the truth!
Col. Jessup: You can't *handle* the truth!

Remember that conversation? It's from the movie *A Few Good Men*, starring Jack Nicholson and Tom Cruise. It's one of my favorite scenes. Why? Because it encompasses the true nature of just about all of us when we search for answers – to whatever the questions might be. In my experience, most people don't really want answers (at least not in the form of truth). Instead, *most people want to be told what they want to hear* – you know, whatever helps them sleep better at night. And to them, if that means "the world is flat," then so be it.

I, on the other hand, would rather know the truth, deal with the consequences, and improve myself (whether it's with my fitness, education or, yes, relationships with others).

Having said that, allow me to share with you a few relationship "truths" of my own, others have shared with me over the years. I admit, I have struggled with some of these in the past, but perhaps you'll fare better than I did when I first learned of these and use them as a foundation to build upon, rather than one to be buried under.

Can you handle these 10 truths? Let's find out …

1. **LOVERS** – If the status of your relationship could be listed as, "It's complicated," then you've got the wrong person. Move on.

2. **LADIES** – Don't believe the myth … Men don't want a woman who's "A lady in the streets but a freak in the sheets." Men just want a freak. Period. (Yes … as in a woman who's crazy sexually in bed … in a *good* way.) Anything outside the sheets (lady-like or otherwise) just makes you that much more interesting. ☺

3. **GENTLEMEN** – The reason most kids' heroes are all on TV is because they can't find any in the home. Be a real man worth looking up to. If the child is yours, take responsibility and be the father you wish YOU had!

4. **LOVERS** – Find someone who celebrates you instead of someone who tolerates you. (Yes, I know … the sex may be great. But what about the other 23 hours of the day?)

5. **LADIES** – If you say, "There aren't any good men/women around worth dating," what you're really saying is, "All I am attracting are men/women who aren't any good." So what's that say about you? (Remember – you get what you give.)

6. **GENTLEMEN** – Do NOT let your mother control your marriage. She had 18+ years to prepare you. Either she did or she didn't.

7. **LOVERS** – A man will tell a woman he loves her so she'll have sex with him. A woman will have sex with a man so he'll fall in love with her. Either way, both parties are f*cked.

8. **LADIES** – A man making $25,000 a year with a vision to make more is wealthier than a man making $50,000 a year with a job and no vision at all. Ten years from now, one will be making (if lucky) slightly more than $50,000 a year. The other will be his boss.

9. **GENTLEMEN** – You can't expect your girlfriend to look like a Victoria's Secret model or your boyfriend to look like an Abercrombie model, yet refuse to shop there for her or him. (Stop being so damn cheap!)

10. **LOVERS** – Research shows couples who *don't* have a TV in their bedroom have 50 percent more sex. Get rid of the TV … *NOW.*

And you're welcome.

-MJ Wilson

Two Sisters, Seven Excuses, And Dr. Phil

The success we want so desperately in our future is often trapped behind the fear we continue to tolerate from our past

---

Twin sisters argue about heading out to an exercise class at the gym:

RACHEL – It's too cold outside.

REBECCA – We work out *inside*. The gym has heat ya know.

RACHEL – (as she plops down on the couch in front of the TV) But traffic will be bad. We'll miss the first 10 minutes of class.

REBECCA – Then let's plan on leaving 15 minutes early.

RACHEL – Yeah but I don't know anybody at the gym.

REBECCA – One: Because you don't go. Two: You know *me*. And three: Who cares?

RACHEL – (pulling the blanket off the chair and over her body) Okay, but right now I'm too tired. Let's go tomorrow.

REBECCA – That's because you never go! Working out gives you energy.

RACHEL – What if I don't know the songs or routines? I'll be embarrassed.

REBECCA – We can stand in the back of the room. Nobody will see us!

RACHEL – What about Caleb? Who's going to pay for a babysitter?

REBECCA – The gym has FREE childcare for its members! Remember? You're already covered.

RACHEL – (sitting up, throwing the blanket off) Ugh! It's easy for you to go to the gym. You're always in a good mood – it's no wonder you work out all the time. But me … I just can't seem to get motivated. I don't know what the problem is.

REBECCA – (nodding her head) I could tell you what your problem is.

RACHEL – Oh really? Well please, "Miss Know-It-All," don't hold back. Tell me … what's wrong with me???

REBECCA – (with a surprised look on her face) Seriously? 'Cause I'd love to.

RACHEL – Yes! *Please.* Share your wisdom with me, "Dr. Phil." Let's put that psych degree of yours to work.

REBECCA – Fine. 'Cause you *need* to hear this. (She pushes her glasses up on her nose and straightens herself, clearing her throat.)

The reason you "can't seem to get motivated" is because you're **apathetic** – you have no real interest in working out. So you don't.

The reason you're apathetic is because you're **depressed** – which makes you feel "blah" and careless, keeping you from wanting to go.

The reason you're depressed is because you're **overweight** – therefore, you don't like your shape, size or the extra pounds you've gained over the last few years. And you definitely don't feel sexy. So the last thing you want to do is be seen at the gym.

The reason you're overweight is because you eat too much junk food and "**comfort food**" – foods that trigger a release of dopamine in your body, giving you a feeling often associated with a pleasurable experience, *like sex*. This has become your new "substitute for love" and now that you're single, you can't get enough.

(At this point Rachel perks up. She's a bit astonished and somewhat impressed with her sister's diagnosis. She begins listening much more intently. Rebecca continues.)

The reason you eat comfort foods and seek a feeling associated with a "pleasurable experience" is because you're **miserable and romantically alone** – ever since Eric broke up with you, you've never dated anyone else, or felt "loved" for that matter. Thus, the craving for the sweets.

The reason you're miserable and romantically alone is because **you don't trust anyone anymore** – you've never forgiven Eric (whether he asks you to or not), or allowed your heart to heal. This has made you bitter and even difficult to be around at times – although you never seem to notice.

And finally, the reason you don't trust anyone anymore and won't let your heart heal is because you're **too afraid to take the risk of falling in love again** and perhaps getting hurt.

It's a downward spiral and it works like a domino effect. One domino falls knocking over another and another… until they all fall down.

So you see? Going to the gym is the beginning of turning all that around. And *that* scares you … because it might mean opening your heart again.

Am I making sense?

RACHEL – (after a long pause and silence, beginning to tear up) I don't know what to say.

I'm so mad at you right now … *and amazed*. I want to punch you in the face and hug you all at the same time. How did you figure all that out?

REBECCA – Let's not focus on that right now. Let's just focus on what *really* matters …

RACHEL – Like what? (as she forms a slight frown) Getting me to go to the gym with you? *STILL?* C'mon Rebecca, gimme a break!

REBECCA – No. (as she grabs Rachel's hand) Like standing up your dominoes again. Because as much as you believe I love the gym, *I love you, even more*.

-Rebecca / Jackson, MS

What Idiot Came Up With This Idea?

There's nothing worse than being involved in an activity, process or system that has been set up and constructed by people who aren't the ones who will actually use it

When I was in my mid-20s, I worked for a clothing store in Parkersburg, WV, just a across the Ohio River from where I grew up. After having been a salesman there for nearly four years, I had become an expert on the store's products and procedures and managed to get a true feel of what worked and what didn't – not only in the store, but in my hometown, too.

Although I hadn't worked there *that* long, I had managed to earn the title of "Top Seller in the Store" numerous times, and was the top seller in our region twice. (Not bad, considering all I had was a high school diploma at the time.)

One day, after finishing the month with my most successful December sales (and the most successful sales month my particular store had ever had … *ever*), I arrived early to find something I had never seen in our store before – a display kit unused and unopened, sent straight from the "big wigs" in Chicago, full of instructions for whomever the lucky fool was to put it all together. It even came with packing slip and "A note from the Top" (whatever the hell that means – as if the rest of us are 'on the bottom'?) and my name roughly scribbled on the side of the box in my manager's hard-to-read handwriting.

"What's this?" I asked her.

"Oh that …" she replied, "You're gonna love it! It's our new display for the front of the store. It's going to promote and showcase our Slim Fit jeans."

"Our Slim Fit jeans? What about our Carpenter jeans?"

"Oh, those are getting moved to the back of the store," she replied.

"Well what idiot came up with this idea?" I shot back.

To which the only reply I got was a quick "Ours is not to wonder why, ours is but to do or die." She then handed me the instructions and told me, "Read these ASAP." (Apparently, *I* had become the "lucky fool.")

Now at this point you may be wondering why I was being such a close-minded jerk about things. I mean … it's not like I was the manager. And I certainly didn't own the store. So what's the problem, right?

Well let me tell ya … The problem was, I was good at my job. *Really good.* I had a pattern. A system. A *knack*. Things were working and working well for me. Replacing our middle-priced Carpenter jeans in the front of our store with our very expensive Slim Fit jeans was sure to hurt my sales dramatically. Why? Because our Slim Fit jeans lacked something of great value and purpose that our Carpenter jeans did not: a *hammer holder loop*. (Google it if you don't know.)

"Why did this matter?" you ask?

You ever been to Parkersburg, WV?

Parkersburg (and the Mid-Ohio Valley for that matter) was, and still is, a hardworking, rural type of town. We've never been afraid to get our hands dirty to change the motor in our car or add a lift-kit to our truck. We'll work in the January snow or the July heat just to shingle a roof, build a shed or even a brand-new home if necessary. That hammer holder loop, as simple as it is, makes work like this (and a lot of other things) that much easier. So having those Carpenter jeans visible in the front of my store as shoppers walked by was critical for me. For every pair of our Slim Fit jeans I sold, I sold four pairs of our Carpenter jeans. Not because they were cheaper (although that didn't hurt), but because of that damn hammer holder loop! Hell I had two pair myself for that very reason!

And putting that display in the front and my Carpenter jeans in the back meant the difference between me simply having a job and me having "Top Seller" status and commissions. But I couldn't seem to get that point across to my manager.

Needless to say, my sales (and the store's) declined dramatically that month, and continued to do so, as we received more and more "expert" directions "from the Top." Within a year I was gone. Within two, so was the store.

My point? The next time your bosses comes to you with "A note from the Top" and some dumbass idea telling you how to improve your job – written by someone who has never actually done it and never will – please, share *my* story with them. And then tell them to go screw themselves.

I'M JOKING, I'm joking! (Although it would feel pretty good, wouldn't it?)

But seriously … if this happens to you, I highly advise you to start looking for a new job. 'Cause working in a place that takes directions from someone who has never done your job and never will is a pretty good indication you're going to need one soon.

-James / Pittsburgh, PA

Buried Alive

*Sometimes you have to bury people
long before they ever die*

What started out as a small touch of his hand on mine during a chance meeting, blossomed into a full-blown affair two months later. He was married. *I was married.* It was so, so wrong I know, but it felt so right.

What had I done? This just wasn't me. After 30 years of marriage, I was supposed to be a happy grandmother, swapping photos of my grandbabies with my girlfriends while finishing up Bible study on an early Wednesday morning. But me? I couldn't get *him* … Kenneth, off my mind. I had to do something.

After meeting with him for nearly three months, I decided to call it off. Not because I didn't absolutely love every minute with him. Believe me, I soaked up every second. He made me feel like what I always imagined Cinderella must've felt like at the ball – like nobody else in the world mattered. It was heavenly. But when it was over, I couldn't look at myself in the mirror anymore.

I felt so ashamed. Dirty. *Bad.*

Besides the guilt I felt towards my husband, family and church, I also felt extremely ashamed towards God. It was slowly killing me inside. The experience may have felt heavenly, but the guilt was hell on Earth.

Two years and several, several prayers later, I hadn't felt much relief in my heart but had managed to remain faithful to my husband. Had he forgiven me? I never told him. Had God? I suppose so … At least that's what I believed. But had I forgiven myself? *That* was the question. I hadn't seen Kenneth since I called it off. But in my mind I saw him every day.

What do I do? How can I move on? Is he out there somewhere thinking of me, too? These are the questions I rehearsed over and over in my mind, until one day, all that changed with one phone call.

"Hey, how are you?"

It was my sister. She had called just to say hi. As I began to reply, my voice cracked a little and I managed to squeak out a fragile "I'm okay. How are you?" Right then and there she knew something was wrong and she didn't have to press me hard to find out. Before she could even ask, I began to cry. I then confessed and cried some more. And after a three-hour conversation and several tears shared by both of us, she said the most profound thing I had ever heard.

"Sis … Sometimes you have to bury people long before they ever die."

Her words pierced my heart.

"In real life," she continued, "when someone we love passes, what do we do? Do we just 'call it off' and walk away? Do we act like they never existed? Like they never made us laugh or cry or feel or live? Of course not! That would make no sense. But at the same time, we also don't keep them around, either. That would be disrespectful. They *have* passed. They *are* gone. And if we don't deal with them and death properly, things can get really nasty. Burial isn't just a nice thing to do … It's necessary."

I was speechless. I had never thought of it this way.

"Mary, you've got to bury him. You know … Have your own mental, emotional, soul-wrenching, heart-bending 'funeral' and be done with it. Think of what you want to say to him as if he really is there and really has passed, and say it. Get it out of your system … all of it. Cry as hard as you must, but get it out. And when you're done and you've said all you know and feel, turn around and walk away. Life goes on, and you will, too."

That was four years ago to this day that I had that conversation with my sister, and tomorrow will be exactly four years to the day that I (emotionally) had my funeral for Kenneth.

Do I still think of him from time to time? *Of course I do.* However, when I do, three little words come to my mind (and heart) that have been said so many times at so many funerals …

"Rest in peace."

Because I laid my relationship with Kenneth to rest then, I can honestly say, I am truly resting in peace now.

-Mary / Charlotte, NC

My Co-Workers Annoy The Hell Outta Me!

Sometimes we don't need a bigger belt.
Sometimes we just need a smaller waist

Dear MJ,

I'm a 27-year-old female with a college degree, good looks, no kids and I'm not married (enjoying the single life for now!) I've got a nice car, great apartment and practically no debt. Everything's great in my life except for one thing ...

I hate my job.

My alarm goes off at 7 a.m. and I immediately wish it were 5 p.m. so I could already be back home, doing something else. Anything else. I want to quit my job so badly it hurts.

Why?

Well part of it's because it's not what I want to do ... at least not exactly. Like so many college students, I went to school for one thing, but ended up changing my major and doing another. So that's some of it. But the MAIN reason I hate my job is because of my co-workers – THEY ANNOY THE HELL OUTTA ME!

They never seem to do what they're told, they're always late or calling off, they don't listen to instructions and they work like they're in slow motion! It's unbelievable. It's like I'm the only one who knows what to do and how to do it – which means I end up doing my job AND theirs!

Why do I have to do the work of TWO people if I'm getting paid as only one???

It's such bullsh*t.

Regardless of how good the rest of my life is, this job situation seems to be ruining everything else! Believe me … I can't wait until the day when I can quit, walk out that door for the last time and never look back!

It's sad. Really sad. And I hate it. But I don't know what to do.

How can I make my co-workers change?

- Whitney / St. Louis, MO

Dear Whitney,

I will tell you the same thing a friend of mine told me years ago: "You can work with anthrax if you have the right suit on."

What I mean is, it's not *who* you're working with, it's how you prepare yourself to work with them! All this time you've been blaming your co-workers for your misery, but the truth is, *you can't expect more out of the people you interact with in life, than the level at which you're willing to interact with them on!* (You may have to read that a couple times slowly to let it sink in. And please do.)

Let me give you an example: Let's say you were a freshman in college and you were (for whatever reason) going to be eating lunch with your little brother at his elementary school today. What do you think that lunch period would be like? Civil? Quiet? Do you think your little brother and his classmates would have the same conversations and interactions as you and your college peers in your university's student lounge? Of course not! And why? *Because you and your college peers are on a different level than*

81

they are! Socially, mentally, emotionally … even maturity-wise. If you tried to interact with those elementary students on *your* level, you would quickly become frustrated, annoyed, and after a while, even exhausted. At some point you'd have to realize it's not that they're so far behind, but that *you're so far ahead*. You and they are simply on different levels.

Keeping that example in mind, let's look at your co-workers. And please know, I'm NOT saying they're not annoying as hell, 'cause believe me, I've known several people who have been right where you are and I couldn't agree with you more. (If you've ever seen the movie "Office Space," I'm sure you'll agree.) However, has it ever dawned on you that when it comes to your co-workers, just like those elementary students, you really *aren't* like them?

You DO listen to directions.
You DO have a great work ethic.
You DO give your best every day.
You DON'T call off all the time.
You DON'T work in slow motion.

And sure, we can easily say, "Well maybe they need to pick up the pace a little bit, too! Raise their standards! Improve their efforts! They're NOT elementary students – they should be able to do this just like me!" Right? But the truth is, just because they should, it doesn't mean they will (obviously).

Listen … I feel for you. I really do. I have been in this exact same position several times in my life and it truly sucks. HOWEVER … (Don't you hate it when people say that? LOL) as I look over my past jobs and positions where this was the case, I now can clearly see my co-workers weren't really the problem, but rather, the product of a much bigger one …

I was unhappy with how little I had accomplished with how much time I'd been given.

In other words, I felt like I should've been further along by then. With my degree, experience and work ethic, I felt I should've been higher up in the ranks, making a lot more money, having those people working FOR me, not WITH me.

Does that make sense?

Taking this viewpoint with this understanding will greatly increase your chances of improving your situation (I know it did for me!), but *you have to act upon it.* Wanting it or even needing it isn't enough. You've got to do something about it.

"Like what?" you ask?

Like taking a serious look at *who* you are, *where* you are, and *what* you want to be doing for the next 30 or 40 years. You may need to start looking for a new job in a field that you believe you will be happy. Or go back to school and add to your degree. (I know you probably don't wanna hear that, but two or three more years of school to get nearly 40 years of a profession you love would be well worth it!) You could (and should) start planning out the rest of your life (long-term) and where you specifically want to be in the next 3 to 5 years (short-term).

And most importantly, teach yourself to work with people at any level, realizing it's not what *they* do to you, it's how *you* respond to them. That's what makes all the difference.

Remember, anyone can expect more from others. That's easy. But if you really want to see a change in your life, you're going to have to expect more from yourself.

-MJ Wilson

The Odd-Model Couple

*The struggle to get out of it can't be any worse
than the pain of staying in it*

We were married for nearly seven years. Had two beautiful children, big house, nice yard, dog, cat, even a goldfish. We both had great jobs, nice cars, and took expensive family vacations every summer. We were loved by many in the community and were the envy of even more – a "Model Couple" of sorts, with that "this is what marriage is supposed to look like" perception.

Did we fight? At first, yes. Don't all couples? But towards the end, no. We eventually just learned to stay out of each other's way.

Sex? Occasionally when we were first married, but once we had our kids we just stopped. (He slept in the spare bedroom during our last three years together.)

Money? I eventually had my own account, he had his. No big deal.

So what happened? Why did we split up?

Because we were miserable together.

We were married too soon; we were too young and too unprepared. We had no idea what we were getting into and it hurt. We had become comfortable with being uncomfortable – no longer the "model couple," but rather a couple modeling a lie … and that's a dangerous place to be.

Once you accept this as your fate (the acceptance that your life will never be what it could be, living like actors in your own relationship, reading the lines and going through the motions), your life will begin a slow spiral into an abyss of unhappiness, bitterness and hate. And we both refused to allow that to happen to either of us.

"But what about the kids?" you ask. "Don't you want to be there for them?"

And I ask you, "Are we not?"

Just because Aaron and I no longer live under the same roof, it in no way implies that our kids don't matter to us! If anything the kids are better off now than before. Why?

Because it's better to come from a broken home than to be in one.

Instead of our kids growing up with two amazing but miserable parents who despise each other, modeling unhappiness, resentment and a fake love, our kids are growing up with two amazingly happy parents who have both moved on, found someone else who makes them the happiest they've ever been, and are no longer living a lie.

That, to me, is a couple worth modeling.

-Julie / Milwaukee, WI

I Swear, If You Ask Me That One More Time ...

Those who can, do. Those who can't,
annoy those who can

Okay, before you jump into this story, you have to know the background that comes with it. So check this out ...

I sent this story off to Fred (my editor), so he could proofread it. Normally, I get these stories back with a ton of red marks for using improper grammar, etc., but nothing major. However, this time his feedback was *quite* different. Different enough that I thought it was worth sharing.

This is literally, word-for-word, what he sent back to me:

> *Wilson – What does this section serve as? I know it shows how rude people can be to ask these questions (and points out other faults they have) ... but some of the responses are pretty mean-spirited. Now don't get me wrong: I enjoy the sass throughout this. And I do see the value in the comic relief this section provides. But most of your vignettes provide life lessons – points for readers to ponder.*
>
> *Do these responses fit with the theme of your book?*
>
> *(Just wanted you to ruminate on the purpose here.)*

After I read Fred's comments, I'd like to say that I took his advice and corrected everything accordingly. But truth be told, the first thing I did was look up the word "ruminate" to see what it means! (Hey, I may have a master's degree, but it's not like I say "ruminate" on a daily basis, here!) After doing so (and laughing at myself in the process), I found that it means, *"to reflect deeply on a subject."*

Okay, so Fred wants me to "reflect deeply" on this story and perhaps think twice about adding it to the Beef Stew stories, right? (Or at a minimum, at least know why I'm adding it.) And after much thought (or ruminating!) I decided the purpose of this story is to show you, the reader, that you are not alone when it comes to being asked annoying questions. We all get them and we all wanna punch the people who ask them right in the throat, right? (Okay, maybe not literally, but you can't tell me you haven't thought about it at least once!)

So here's your comic relief. A survey of nine of the most annoying questions we all hear, along with the brilliant and sometimes sarcastic answers suggested by a few of my friends from across the country.

Feel free to "ruminate" over these the next time *you* wanna punch someone right in the throat! And although they're not to be taken too seriously, always remember: There's typically a little bit of truth in even the simplest joke. So pay attention!

P.S. #7 and #9 are *my* favorites! I about choked on my food when I read them.

Annoying Question #1
HOW MUCH MONEY DO YOU MAKE?

Answer: *Apparently not enough or I wouldn't still be hanging out with you.* Listen honey, it's none of your business how much money I make. Besides, why do you want to know? What are you possibly going to do with this information? Help me invest? Perhaps donate to my child's college fund? *Yeah right.* You and I both know the only reason you wanna know how much money I make is so you'll know how much you wanna borrow from me!

I'm sorry I worked so hard for my financial status. Had I known sitting on my ass and doing nothing while waiting for "Mr. Right" to show up was a career choice, perhaps we'd both be on the same busted-up playing field right now.

-Michelle / Washington, D.C.

Annoying Question #2
YOU MEAN YOU'RE *STILL* NOT MARRIED YET?

Answer: You mean you're still not divorced yet? Listen, just because you're in a miserable marriage and don't have the guts to get out, it doesn't mean I need to rush into a marriage so you can feel better about yours. I'm in no hurry to "settle down" like you.

I'm single, not desperate.

-Tyler / Omaha, NE

Annoying Question #3
SHOULDN'T YOU BE DONE WITH YOUR DEGREE BY NOW?

Answer: IT'S A FOUR-YEAR PROGRAM! And that's only if I go full-time – which I'm not, because I can't! I'm barely into year number three! YOU try working 40 hours a week, managing two kids AND going back to school. *It ain't easy.*

And don't be hatin' on me either! Just because you dropped out and never went back doesn't mean I can't go back or won't finish! I WILL finish and I WILL graduate. I don't care if it takes me 10 years! Just remember, we aren't getting any younger. And at our age, I think the only one falling behind in this scenario is YOU.

-Shannon / Des Moines, IA

Annoying Question #4
DIDN'T YOU ALREADY TRY THIS DIET ONCE BEFORE?

Answer: And? Is there something wrong with trying it again? Maybe I feel more confident this time. Maybe I feel better about the plan. Maybe I failed the first time and wanna try again. At least I'm trying, which is better than doing *nothing* about my weight, or my looks, or my career ... *like you.*

-Tonya / Dover, DE

Annoying Question #5
WHEN ARE YOU TWO GONNA HAVE SOME BABIES? DON'T YOU WANT CHILDREN?

Answer: We will have babies WHEN we want babies, IF we want babies! And we're certainly not having them for you! Just because you had all four of your children by the time you were 26 doesn't mean we're falling behind. We want to live as a couple FIRST and as parents second. We may wait until we're both over 30. Maybe 35. Maybe not at all. But believe me, if and when we do have babies, trust me, you'll be the first one ... no scratch that ... we'll probably *never* tell you. Seriously.

-Mitchell & Nicole / Minneapolis, MN

Annoying Question #6
WHY ARE YOU STILL SMOKING? DON'T YOU KNOW IT'S BAD FOR YOU?

Answer: Gee ... let me think for a minute ... Wow. *No. I did not know smoking was bad for me. I had no idea.* All this time wasted. If I had only known, perhaps I could've easily overcome my ADDICTION TO NICOTINE and the feeling of "escape" that my cigarette gives me when people like YOU come around, asking me stupid, annoying questions!

Of course I know it's bad for me.

But rather than remind me CONSTANTLY, why don't you try to understand why I do it? Has it ever occurred to you that maybe I actually DO wanna quit, and have a plan to do so in my own time? It's a lot harder than you think.

If you're truly concerned, why don't you try helping me find a solution to this problem instead of simply telling me the result if I don't?

-Levi / Memphis, TN

Annoying Question #7
YOU LOOK TIRED. ARE YOU OKAY?

Answer: Oh yeah ... I'm good. I was just up all night with your mom.

-Miguel / Albuquerque, NM

Annoying Question #8
ARE YOU *STILL* WORKING THAT BUSINESS? WEREN'T YOU SUPPOSED TO BE RICH BY NOW?

Answer: Are you *STILL* working 40 hours a week at a job you hate? At least I'm doing something about my financial state instead of making fun of others'. You're so busy comparing where I am to where you are ... Why don't you compare where I'm headed to where you'll be?

Oh wait ... I'm sorry. I forgot. That might require admitting one of us is following his dream while the other is just dreaming.

-Scott / Seattle, WA

Annoying Question #9
DO YOU HAVE ANY CASH I CAN BORROW? I'M BROKE UNTIL NEXT WEEK.

Answer: Oh my gosh! YOU? BROKE??? NO WAAAAY! I just can't believe it! Seems like just the other day you were … No, wait … you're right. You ARE broke. Broke-minded, broke lifestyle, broke friendships.

Let me ask you, when are you *not* broke? You know damn well you and I make the same amount of money. We were hired on the same day and work at the same call center. The only difference between you and me is you blow your money trying to keep up an image you can't afford (Miss "Fake it 'til you make it") while I save my money trying to live within my means.

Stop buying new shoes every week. Stop buying a new cell phone every six months. And stop blaming the Devil every time your electric gets cut off. Last time I checked it was your jobless, classless, live-in boyfriend who was taking all your money, *not Satan.*

-Kelsey / Denver, CO

And The Winner Is …

Sometimes it takes longer to get to the Starting Line than it does to the Finish Line

---

We've all heard one or more of these inspiring stories …

Oprah Winfrey, one of the wealthiest and most influential women of all-time, was born in rural Mississippi to a teenage single mother and was so poor growing up she often wore dresses made from potato sacks. **Walt Disney** was once fired from a job for "lacking imagination and good ideas." **J.K. Rowling**, one of the best-selling authors of all time (*Harry Potter*), was once advised by an editor to "get a day job" based upon the belief that Rowling's books would never sell. And even **Jack Canfield**, co-author of *Chicken Soup for the Soul* and my inspiration to write *this* book, was rejected more than 140 times by publishers who informed him "Anthologies just don't sell."

Yes, these stories, and many others just like them, are amazing, inspiring, and more importantly, *true*. But do they *really* inspire *us*? Do we truly allow the feelings of failure or being misunderstood, the countless rejections, or the understanding of what it feels like to simply be told "you're not good enough" really sink into our own conscious and cause us to try that much harder to reach our own goals? I don't think so (or at least not to the degree that I think we should). And I think I know why.

Most of us are working 40 or more hours a week (or even working two jobs) just to make ends meet. We're married with kids, or divorced with kids, or starting our next marriage. We hold college degrees that we seemingly can't use and still have a place in our heart for our first love (although we married someone else). We've had the multi-level marketing businesses come and go, relatives pass unexpectedly, and if truth be told, we sometimes wonder if God actually exists (although we'd never admit it). We take our kids to soccer practice, fix dinner, do laundry, shovel the snow or mow the lawn, and on occasion, when we get some free time (IF we get free time!), we usually are so tired all we want to do is collapse on the couch and watch TV.

With so much on our plates (and minds) it's no wonder the idea of becoming the next great sports athlete or literary phenom isn't exactly a top priority. We just want to make it through the day with no emergency room visits, phone calls from the principal, or flat tires. An inspiring story for us doesn't have to be of "rock star status." It may just be something as simple as one of us getting a job promotion, or staying married long enough to see our 10th wedding anniversary.

You know, something *we* can relate to …

Justin – flunked 7th grade and dropped out after 9th. Has never met his father. Mother is a drug addict. Older brother in prison (drugs), and younger brother, juvenile detention (theft, drugs). Justin was often beaten by his mother's live-in boyfriends while growing up, and was constantly subjected to drug abuse. Never having a true family to call his own, by all accounts Justin should be (at least statistically) abusive, in prison, addicted to or selling drugs, or dead. But that's not the case … Wanna take a guess what he's doing now?

Justin, just shy of his 30th birthday, is a happily married father of four, has a full-time job that he loves, is currently working on his G.E.D., believes his wife is the best thing that's ever happened to him (besides his own children), and is one of the most generous, caring husbands and fathers I've ever met.

He may have come from a "failed" family, and he may not be rich or famous, but he *is* living *his* dream – to be a faithful husband, a father involved in his children's lives, and a provider for and producer of one of the best families anyone could ever ask for.

How's *that* for inspiration? Need more?

Abigail – a Hispanic minority and eldest of three children growing up in a single-parent home. To this day, she's never met her father.

Her mother worked two jobs just to pay rent. Abigail, pregnant by the age of 16, was a teen *and* mother at the same time. Having to provide for two (and still help her mom and younger brothers), she found money scarce. She would often feed her daughter cereal with water (because they had no milk) or go without food altogether just so her daughter and brothers could eat. She would wear men's clothing donated by a neighbor, and walk nearly four miles to work when she couldn't get a ride. At one point, she was even using old socks as washcloths when taking a bath, and working the night shift at a local grocery store just so her mother could watch her daughter.

Forget living paycheck-to-paycheck. Abigail was living day-to-day.

And again (at least according to statistics), Abigail should be ... well, I'm sure you can imagine where and what Abigail *should* be by now. So let's just focus on where she is now.

Today, Abigail is a recent college graduate (with honors) at the age of 31. She works full-time and, as she puts it, "now has a career instead of a job." Her daughter is a 10th grade honor roll student and a varsity volleyball player (future scholarship most likely). They live in their new apartment, in a nice, quiet neighborhood, located in a top-notch school district. Abigail is currently dating a fellow graduate and hopes to eventually start her own online business.

Isn't *that* beautiful???

More importantly, isn't that inspiring?

It's never about what happens to us in life, but rather, it's how we respond. Justin and Abigail aren't famous athletes or bestselling authors. They're everyday people living next to you and me who are doing the best they can to turn their bad situations into good ones.

Regardless of where you were born or how you were raised, who walked out on you or what they did to you, what you've been told or what you believe, you _can_ turn things around. _Everyone's in a different place, but we're all in the same race_ (it's called "life"). And the question when you die won't be, "What place did you finish?" (That's the myth that so many of us have fallen for. And that's just not what it's about.) The real question will be, "Did you finish or did you quit?"

Your answer to that question alone will determine your future _despite_ your past.

Just ask Justin or Abigail.

-MJ Wilson

The Forever-Single Church Lady

Just because your house is empty, doesn't mean it's on the market. Ya gotta put up a "For Sale" sign!

Dear Miss Debra,

I need your help! With you being co-leader of our singles ministry, you know that I'm a God-loving, God-fearing woman. I attend church three times per week, choir practice every Tuesday night, and haven't missed a singles meeting in six months – even though none of the men there are of my liking! I don't drink, smoke or cuss, and I faithfully attend our women's Bible study once a week. I work full-time and support myself. I feel like I am a good catch for any man, yet at 44 years of age, I am still unmarried and haven't been asked out on a date in years.

All I want is an honest, faithful man – with a decent job, of course – who loves the Lord and is ready to settle down! Is that too much to ask? What am I doing wrong? I only ask you because I know you have a successful marriage and I trust you. I know you won't tell me what I want to hear, you'll tell me what I need to hear. So please, fire away! I'm all ears.

-Rhonda

Dear Rhonda,

Thanks for reaching out! I'm happy to help! However, let me remind you that YOU said "fire away," not me! So please keep that in mind as you read my reply and I'll tell you exactly what you need to hear. ☺

First of all, you state that you are a God-loving, God-fearing woman – great! But are you a man-loving, man-fearing woman? (And I don't mean "fearing" as in afraid, but in reverence or respect.) Do you respect men? All you seem to have stated is how much you attend church and love God. However, if I were to ask the average "godly" man to state what he loves or is about, do you think I'd get the same answer? Probably not. At some point I think (in addition to loving God) he'd also list things like classic cars or college football, barbecues or going to the beach. You know ... things that show his "flavor" or what he's like. What are some things that *you* love that could show *your* flavor? Things men might love as well? Showing these things and sharing them with those around you will increase your appeal.

Second, let's talk about your tardiness! (Hey girl – you knew I'd be REAL with you – that's why you wrote me!) You and I both know you are consistently 20 minutes (or more) late for church every week! What message do you think this is sending any man who may be interested in asking you out? (Date her and be late to everything you go to? Especially something as important as church?) It's just not attractive and it tells a man you don't have it together.

Besides arriving late, you often leave early, too. How's a man to get to know you, let alone ask you out if there's no time for him to do so? He certainly isn't going to do it during the service! (And if he does, that is sooo wrong you need to get up and find another seat AND man!)

Finally, let's talk about your attendance. You say you attend our church and the singles meetings faithfully, which is great, but do you ever attend other functions? Places where men (yes, *godly* men) are likely to be in attendance? Like sporting events or concerts, maybe a festival downtown, a community gathering, or even your local gym? These are great ways to socialize, make new friends and meet new people. (Contrary to popular belief, *just because you don't meet your man in church, it doesn't mean he doesn't love God!* – I met my Larry at a pumpkin festival of all places, so you never know.)

Can you meet your future husband at church? Of course! But trying to … well that's a different story. Trying to meet your future mate at church is like trying to meet him at the movies: possible, but difficult. Why? Because the focus is not on you (or him) – it's on the presentation (the movie, or in your case, the sermon). And please note, I'm NOT saying this needs to change! I'm simply stating that neither are easy places for any man to ask a woman out to dinner, given the setting and ambience. (How many men do you think feel comfortable singing "Amazing Grace" and then looking over to the woman sitting in the pew next to them and asking, "Hey … You come here often?" *Think about it.*)

And as for the singles ministry – please realize, it is *not* a dating service (and I say that in all kindness). Its goal is not to "hook people up" or to ensure they find their mate. It's simply designed to allow unmarried adults a chance to meet others in similar situations, in hopes that friendships will be made and a sense of "family" will be felt. Anything beyond that (dating or otherwise) is up to the individuals.

Listen, you're not a bad person and you're definitely not a bad catch! You are a beautiful lady and have a lot to offer *any* man! *Really.* You just gotta put yourself out there, girl! If you truly want my advice, I suggest you step out of your comfort zone a little. Join a bowling league or community volleyball team. Volunteer at the YMCA or attend a festival downtown. Go somewhere that, if a man wanted to ask you out, he could do so without feeling awkward or in poor taste for doing so.

Trust me. You don't have to stop being godly … Just start being available.

-Miss Debra / Houston, TX

Do You See What I See?

Stupidity is like an object in motion: It will stay in motion with the same speed and in the same direction unless acted upon by an external force

Take a quick scroll through your favorite social media site or local community chat room/forum and you'll likely turn up one or more of these problems listed below:

#1 AND WE WONDER WHY THE SCHOOL LEVY NEVER PASSES – My husband and I recently moved here and enrolled our kids in the local school system. Apparently, some moron approved by the board decided to draw up the plans for the new student drop-off zone at our school. This "expert" has us (the parents) in our cars competing with the morning school buses and their drivers for the best place to allow our kids/students to enter the building. It's an accident just waiting to happen (my son was almost hit twice already) and it's extremely difficult to leave once you've dropped your child off due to the traffic jam it causes.

Educated people everywhere and they chose this guy and this design to improve our school?

-Brooke / Arkansas

#2 DUMB IDEA + DUMB DECISION = DUMB RESULTS – It's one of our community's busiest intersections. Let's put a gas station and/or pharmacy on *each* of the four corners. Then, in less than a year, they can all slowly go out of business while competing with one another. Soon after we'll have four unsightly buildings with boards over the windows, dilapidated advertisements and weeds growing all around to add to the "beauty" of our already struggling community.

Oh wait … we did that already … on the next street over.

-Shelby / Kentucky

#3 THE (RICH SCHOOL) MONEY PIT – How about the school district I live in … incredible football fields and sports facilities, a $400 student-athlete annual participation fee, and coaching salaries that dwarf nearby school districts. Yet we're constantly bombarded with school levies, the threat of classes being cut (art, gym, music and band), and we can't get air-conditioning in two of our older elementary schools. Our classrooms are over-crowded, or faculty is under-staffed, and our teachers don't even get a planning period during their workday. To make matters worse, with all that money from the participation fees, somehow we still end up with high-school students "volunteering" as referees to officiate elementary games, and our team "uniforms" (a cheap t-shirt with a number and your child's last name on the back) still costs an *additional* $20!

But don't get me wrong … I'm sure "Education comes FIRST" in our district. I mean, why else would our superintendent get ANOTHER raise???

-Vince / Florida

#4 BASS ACKWARDS BUSINESS – Whatever you do, do NOT let any prominent businesses come into your small town and build a few restaurants or local tourist attractions (especially if you have a town near the water or full of history like ours). No … that would make too much sense. Don't use your brain or anything.

Instead, do what our town did: Take your busiest or most historical street, tear down all major landmarks and cultural icons, and install used-car lots and storage buildings in their place. This way, two local business owners profit a little while the rest of the town suffers greatly.

Absolutely ridiculous.

Our leadership doesn't seem to get it. Remaining a small town doesn't mean remaining a "stuck" town. Despite popular belief, we *can* grow without losing our charm. Don't believe me? Check out Port Townsend, Washington.

-Valerie / Oregon

#5 THE (UNGODLY) GODLY – I've been attending the same church now for the last seven years. One thing I've noticed that increasingly disturbs me is how we *continue* to ask for money for our Building Fund (despite never needing it) and our Community Fund (despite never using it).

Our Building Fund is supposedly in place so we can increase the size of our church (to accommodate its growth when necessary) and the Community Fund is supposedly for community emergencies and/or benefits (relief for local victims of natural disasters, food for the needy, or to help the community in a positive way). Yet for as long as I've been here, we've spent thousands of dollars increasing the *size* of our church – bigger sanctuary, new gymnasium, more seating – despite its lack of growth (we have fewer attendees now than when I started) and we're remodeling our pastor's office … *again!* (This time we're adding on a private kitchen … apparently the break room just down the hall from his office is too far to walk.)

Worse, we still have never done *anything* for the local community! I mean *nothing!* No free oil changes for single moms, no free legal advice for those going through divorce, no lawn service for the elderly, no donations to the local parks and playgrounds, no food pantry, no homeless shelter … *Nothing.*

If you ask me, the question shouldn't be, "What would Jesus do?" The real question is, *"What would Jesus do about what we are not doing?"*

-Carlos / Nevada

#6 ... AND THE FORTY THIEVES – In my city, local police and firefighters are driving police cars and fire trucks that lack modern equipment. These brave men and women risk their lives – burglaries, gang fights, burning buildings – with technology that's outdated or in disrepair. Each year they beg for donations to improve their safety and ours. Yet at the same time, our local and state governments continue to spend thousands and thousands of dollars (taxpayers' dollars I might add) on anything from new leather-bound chairs and oak desks for their offices to limousine services and tickets to the local symphony. (Did I mention this was from taxpayers' money and NOT from their own income?)

Ironically, several of these politicians promised lower crime and increased public safety while running for office. Unfortunately, the only thing that's gotten lower is the amount of money these jerks have to spend out of their own pockets.

-Antonio / California

IN ~~EINSTEIN'S~~ MY OWN WORDS – Regardless of *how* these problems are brought to our attention – sarcastic complaints, social whining or legitimate concern – it doesn't dismiss the fact that these problems are ... well ... *still problems*.

They *do* exist in several of our communities.

They *are* affecting us in a negative way.

And they *can* be reviewed, questioned and or even investigated.

Keeping this in mind, I'd like you to go back and reread each problem I listed previously. (Yes, all six of them.) And when you do, forget about *how* they're told to you and think about *what* they're telling you.

Do they sound familiar? Are any of them happening in your church? Your school district? Your community?

Do you even know?

I don't say that to be rude or condescending. *I'm serious.* Do you even know what's going on in the world around you? Are you aware of what's (possibly) happening right under your nose on a daily basis that's affecting you in a negative way?

I realize most of us have so much going on at any given moment that the last thing we feel like making time for is attending our local school-board meeting, voting in the next town-hall election, or doing a little research to find out where our donations are going.

But maybe we should.

Or if nothing else, the least we could do is start looking around and asking questions. This process doesn't have to be difficult or intense, it just needs to be started.

Let's start questioning our current methods. Let's take a serious look at their validity. And let's investigate who, what, when, where, how and why.

Your city:
- Does it really take a *zillion* orange barrels and two years of road construction to fix a two-mile stretch of road? Seriously? Could there be something else going on here you don't know about?

Your county:
- Am I wrong or isn't the guy running for treasurer in your county the same guy who was caught embezzling thousands of dollars from his previous place of employment? And this doesn't seem a little strange to you?

Your church:
- Do you really need to remodel your offices every 3-5 years? Does the carpet in the sanctuary really need replaced … again? Isn't there a low-income housing community just a few miles away or a local family or two who could desperately use your help – financially or otherwise?

Your local school district:
- Your superintendent got another raise because why??? And who's planning the school budget so poorly that every five years you have to pass *another* levy? Are levies really the *only* way to raise money for schools? Where's all the money from the sports programs going?

Your community:
- Why did they cut down all the trees along the main road? Were they in the way or something? And did your town really need another used car lot or over-sized parking lot put in? Why not a new park, library or public media center? Who made these decisions and why?

Your world:
- You tell me … What's a good question to ask???

Now before you send me an email explaining why your church or school or other "thing" needs whatever I've questioned above, I want you to realize, I did NOT say that these places or organizations *don't* need these things, I *asked* if they do. I honestly don't know what's relevant to your respective area and what's not – that's why I asked. And that's all I'm hoping you'll begin to do – start asking.

Maybe your church *does* need new carpet. Maybe your town *does* need another gas station – I honestly have no idea. Only you can answer those questions and I hope you'll do whatever it takes to do so.

Remember, it only takes one to get the ball rolling.

Don't be afraid to investigate.

Don't be afraid to ask questions.

Or as I started to write at the beginning of my response and will do so now: In the words of Albert Einstein, "The important thing is to not stop questioning."

Pretty simple advice, I know. But it was given to us by a man who became a genius, not because he had all the answers, but because he never stopped looking for them.

And neither should you.

Keep investigating.

Keep asking questions.

And yes, keep looking.

-MJ Wilson

Stuck

Change may start with a belief, but it ends with an action

The following letter was sent to me a few years ago from a former student of mine. Given the subject matter, I wanted to share it in this book. Please note, however, I do so only with his permission, as well as my agreement to change his name and any specific details that may give away his or his family's identity.

Dear Mr. Wilson,

Long time no see, right? I hope you are well.

I remember, years ago when I was in your class, our long talks about life: my problems at home with my stepfather, my worrying about the future, girls, etc. You set me on a good path and I'm grateful. But lately, things aren't so good, and I'm hoping you can help me again since you're the best resource I know.

I've been really depressed lately and I don't know what to do. It's my marriage. It's killing me. It's been 7 years now and nothing seems to be improving.

I should've gotten out 5 years ago when I had the chance. It would've been so much easier then. But now, with a daughter and a mortgage I just don't see how I'll ever be free.

I feel so hopeless. So ... stuck.

I want out. Is that wrong?

As I sit and write this to you, I am reminded of the lyrics to the song "Hurt" that you taught us about in class one time. Remember that one? The version sung by Johnny Cash? I suppose given my circumstances, "Folsom Prison Blues" might seem more appropriate (don't laugh), but these lines (although brief and simple) really speak to me:

"If I could start again, a million miles away
I would keep myself. I would find a way."

That's exactly how I feel. If I could start again I would do things much differently.

I would think before I act (instead of worrying about what everyone else thinks of me).

I wouldn't do something (like getting married) just because all my friends are doing it.

And I definitely wouldn't do something so life-changing – so permanent – just to please my parents. It's just not worth it.

I would keep myself. I would find a way.

But it's too late for me now. I did the deed and now I have to suffer the consequences. There's no going back. And that's why I'm writing you, Mr. Wilson. Maybe you can answer the one question that after 7 years, I cannot:

"How can I ever be happy in my marriage when I'm not in love with my wife and never have been?"

Please help me.

I'll do whatever you tell me. I'm desperate.

Chris

Not only is Chris's letter sad, but unfortunately, very common, too. I've met so many people over the years who seem to be in a similar situation – stuck and hopeless in a miserable relationship.

It doesn't have to be this way. Things *can* change … but like I told Chris, "It might get worse before it gets better."

Let me explain.

I'm not a doctor. But I am a logical man, and fairly well versed, and if there's one thing I know, and have said several times before, it's this:

If you do the same thing today that you did yesterday, you'll find yourself in the same place tomorrow.

I've seen people fight for their marriage, seek counseling and make it work. I've also seen people decide "enough is enough," seek a divorce, and find someone who makes them truly happy. But one thing I have never, ever seen, *not even once*, is someone sit and do nothing about their marriage and it just magically improve.

If you find yourself in a situation similar to Chris's, you have but three options:

1) **GET IN** – Find out why the love just isn't there and do whatever it takes to create it (if possible) or restore it. This may be done through the help of a marriage counselor, therapist or possibly even your pastor or church depending upon your belief system. Just make sure you do it and do it well. Anything done half-assed will just bring you right back to square one.

2) **GET OUT** – Find a good lawyer, follow his or her instructions and get a divorce. Just make sure it's quick and clean. Dragging this process out over stupid things like who gets the second television or the extra mattress is really petty and immature. Besides, it will make you much more bitter and a bit of a monster, and who really wants that?

I realize no one really wants to be divorced, but that doesn't mean you should stay miserably married, either. Just know if you do decide to take this route, don't play around with it. Either do it or don't. But don't make idle threats. Divorce is too serious and dangerous for that. (I think of it like a gun: don't get it out unless you plan to use it and don't aim it at something unless you plan to kill it. Keep this in mind and I think you get the picture.)

3) **GET RUN OVER** – This is the worst option of the three, but believe it or not, one of the most common ones chosen. Why? Because a lot of people don't really want a solution, they just want credit for seeking one. (The actual solution involves action on their part that they don't want to do because of fear, guilt and/or laziness. Therefore, they tend to do nothing.) If you take this option, you don't have to do anything – *it will happen automatically*. Just be warned – you do not have the right to complain for the remainder of your marriage if you choose this option. Choosing to do nothing is still choosing something – you're choosing to stay right where you are, miserable and angry. And if that's the case, you now have no one to blame but yourself. Remember, doing nothing will get you nothing.

Whatever option you choose, own the consequences and make the best of them while moving forward in life. Not because life is it too short to be unhappy, but because it's too long to be miserable.

And by the way, in case you're wondering, Chris is a happily married man today.

Did he work things out with his wife? No. He tried, but she had no interest in changing things or going to marriage counseling. She said everything was Chris's fault, *not hers*. And Chris, realizing you can't force people to change, decided enough was enough. He divorced his wife soon after and even got custody of their 5-year-old daughter (which is rare for men). Six months later, he met Amber. She was fresh out of a similar situation and had two beautiful little girls of her own. They were a perfect match.

Chris instantly became the father Amber's little girls never had and the happy husband he's always wanted to be. Amber instantly became the queen she always deserved to be. Today, the five of them make up one of the happiest families I know.

Perfect story? Probably not … Nobody gets married hoping to be divorced. But perfect ending? Well … what more could you ask for? Chris no longer feels like a prisoner in his own life. Amber doesn't feel abandoned and unwanted.

Both got what they wanted and deserved.

Neither got it without doing something about it.

-MJ Wilson

Giving You The Business

*It's not that you're above them,
it's just that you're beyond them*

So when you started out, there were seven of you, but now there's only you?

Everyone quit but you?

All that talk about starting a business together, changing the world, making millions and living the dream …

And EVERY.
SINGLE.
ONE OF THEM.
QUIT.

And now there's only you.

So what's it gonna be? You gonna quit, too? Is your success dependent on theirs? (If it is, you were doomed from the beginning.)

If I waited for all my friends and partners to do what they said they were going to do, you wouldn't be reading this book now.

I've been doubted, made fun of, judged morally and ethically (a lot of people have their own expectations of how I should live my life and write my books), questioned, ripped off, criticized for my viewpoints (some think I'm "too preachy," others think I don't preach enough), and even lied to by several people – some being my friends.

But none of it ever stopped me.

Why?

Because I'd rather die pursuing my dream than live my life without one.

Do you realize, at this precise moment while I write these words, I'm not exactly where I want to be yet (financially, socially, professionally)? However, I'm also not where I used to be, either (mentally, emotionally, professionally). I LOVE my new life and career choice! I know it's all just a matter of time before my dream comes true and I'm on that "Best-Seller" list!

I don't say that to boast, *I say that because I believe.*

I know it's not easy pursuing your dream, but if you don't, you'll spend the rest of your life working for people who are pursuing theirs.

Listen …

Remind yourself of why you started in the first place.

Remind yourself of all the obstacles you've already overcome just to make it where you are today.

Remind yourself that you *are* different: *You* have the idea. *You* have the passion. *You* want the freedom.

It's not about proving others wrong. It's about proving to yourself you were right. Stop complaining about what they didn't do and start looking at what needs to be done!

It reminds me of the lyrics to an old Kid Rock song:

"All the sh*t we talked, all the sh*t we dreamed, I did it without you, I got a brand new team."

And that's exactly what YOU need to do …

Get a brand new team.

Speak the dream.

And start working towards the life you want, instead of complaining about the one you have.

-MJ Wilson

A Schoolteacher, Some Drunk Guy And Standardized Tests

Just because it's not your fault
doesn't mean it's not your problem

I live in an older apartment complex in a large city. After three years of teaching in my old neighborhood, our school levy didn't pass and I was "let go." In need of a job and eager to get back in the classroom, I accepted a teaching position and residence in a low-income school district as part of an agreement to have a portion of my student loans paid back. I've been here only a week and I'm having second thoughts.

Two days ago, at roughly 2 a.m., I am suddenly awakened by the sound of a very angry man yelling at someone just outside my window.

Being a single, 24-year-old female from the country, I'm a little unsure what I should do. I grew up in a small town smack dab in the middle of nowhere. I'm not used to having someone living right above me and right beside me. (As in their front door is about four feet away from mine – both sides!) I've got to tell you, I'm a little afraid, to say the least.

What if it's a drug deal gone wrong? What if it's gang-related? What if it's a domestic fight? What if they see me?

The shouting continues. So I wait.

After what seems to be a lifetime (but in reality is more like five minutes), everything grows quiet outside. At this point I feel it's safe to peer out my window. I grab the baseball bat I have hidden under my bed. I don't know what I plan on doing with it, but in some weird way it makes me feel braver.

As I peel back my curtains, what I see next doesn't scare me at all ... *it disgusts me.*

It's an older man standing about 10 feet away from my window with his pants around his ankles, urinating in my front yard, while simultaneously chugging his beer!

What the ...? Are you serious?

Now normally I would be so angry I would say something. But in this moment I'm so caught off guard I just stare in disbelief.

What should I do? Call the police? Confront the man? My thoughts are racing. As I contemplate how to handle the situation, he manages to yet amaze me again. Guess what he does next???

This idiot proceeds to take a dump on my sidewalk!!!

WHAT THE HELL???

Where do I live? *And who does this?*

Who takes a dump OUTSIDE in someone else's yard???

As I begin to calm down and think rationally, I decide to call the police and report him. But before I can even find my phone, a car pulls up, the man gets inside, and off he goes. Two minutes later it's so quiet outside you'd never know anything happened.

One minute I have a crazy man outside my door, the next – it's so peaceful I can actually hear a cricket chirping.

Talk about an emotional rollercoaster ...

I get the feeling it's going to be a *long* school year.

Needless to say, I don't think I'm going to sleep well tonight. Thank God it's the weekend and I don't have to teach tomorrow.

Eventually I fall asleep and manage to get a few hours of shut-eye. As the sun comes up and shines through my bedroom window, I decide to assess the damages, if any, that I may have. And oh do I have some!

What I see is even worse than I imagined – my entire yard full of trash, cigarette butts dumped in a pile on my lawn, beer cans between my bushes, and a damp pair of used, men's underwear, crumpled on my steps!

THAT'S. JUST. NASTY.

Absolutely disgusting.

It looks like someone had a house party on my front lawn. It's a total mess.

Talk about being mad. As I look around, I begin to wonder who I can call to clean it up. I mean … I didn't do this. Why should I have to clean it up? Right?

I sit down on my steps and think … cussing in my mind, biting my lip, rubbing my hands together in angst.

In this moment, these words – words I have shared with my students countless times – begin to ring through my head.

"It's not your fault, but it is your problem."

I let out a long sigh and just think. I'm frustrated.

The teacher has become the student again – and I don't like it.

"It's not your fault, but it is your problem?" Believe me, those words are easier to say than to hear.

(Thinking …)

What do I do?

At this point I do what any well-meaning, good-hearted schoolteacher would do: I begin to daydream about all the students I've sent to detention over the years that I wish I could make come to my home right now and clean this mess up!

(You think I'm joking, but I'm not.)

And then, after a laugh or two (and a little bit of grumbling), I roll up my sleeves, put on some gloves and begin to pick up the trash, hose-down my sidewalk and clean the yard myself.

Why?

Because my yard needs cleaned?

Because I hate the sight of all this trash on my lawn?

Because it stinks? (Let's not even go there.)

Of course I do it for those reasons. But those aren't the only reasons.

I also do it because I'm a teacher – I lead by example.

I've always believed that what we do when we're on stage or out in the open doesn't matter nearly as much as what we do when no one's looking ... When there's no reward ... When it's just us. *That's* when our character is truly tested.

Huh ... What a coincidence ...

As a teacher who's mandated to give standardized tests, it seems this time *I* was the recipient of my own "test of standards." And I gotta say ... Based upon the looks of my front lawn – after a little bit of hard work and years of preparation – looks like I passed.

-Amanda / rough part of town, U.S.A.

No ... Seriously. Go Away.
Please.

Stop listening to what they're telling you and start looking at what they're actually giving you

---

Have you seen the sign that some neighborhoods are now posting? The one that says, *"NO SOLICITING – We are too broke to buy anything – We know who we are voting for – and we have found Jesus – Seriously, unless you're selling Thin Mint cookies, Please GO AWAY!!!"*

As funny as this may sound (I got a good laugh out of it the first time I read it, too), it has a lot of truth to it.

The majority of my neighbors and I are well over 50 years of age. We have kids *and* grandkids, which means we're always attending birthday parties, donating to the kids' soccer teams, helping with rent or covering somebody's school loan. We have money, yes. But we have family and they have needs, and bills, and "life."

We have our educations and political sense, and have had them for quite some time. We know how to vote, when to vote and who we want to vote for. And despite your judgments, we consider ourselves to be good people, if not Godly people.

We've seen and heard just about everything. And after 50+ years on this planet, one thing we typically don't see is the action to back up the statement.

So rather than coming to our doors, telling us what we should be doing, buying, saving or giving, how 'bout you show us instead?

For instance …

1) **Stop telling us we need to buy your products, try your services or donate to your cause** – If you're so interested in getting our money, why not demonstrate how you spend yours? SHOW US where you've paid the rent for someone less fortunate. SHOW US where you've given away gas cards or free groceries to a needy family. SHOW US where you've sponsored a local student so that he or she can afford to play sports. *Anything* that would cause us to believe giving our earned income to you would be better than keeping it ourselves. You do *that,* and not only would we be more willing to give, but we might actually buy your products, too.

2) **Stop telling us who to vote for** – If you know who we should vote for then obviously you know our property taxes are too high, the police are under-staffed, and the school levy never passes. So why not take the time you're wasting going door-to-door asking for our votes/support, and instead, use it to find a way to solve one or more of the problems I just listed above. You do *that* and we just might vote for you or your candidate next election.

3) **Stop telling us we need to go to your church** – Has it ever dawned on you that just because we don't go to *your* church, it doesn't mean we don't go at all? Rather than wasting money on catchy fliers and large billboards telling us why we need to come to your house of worship, why don't you stop coming to ours, and instead, do what Jesus did (or would do) – you know … feed the hungry (donate food to a poor family in our community), heal the sick (or at least pay someone's medical bills), offer free school supplies for low-income families, or find a young man trying to better his life through college and help him afford a

tutor or financial aid. (Do I really need to tell you the problems we all face?) Stop telling us what to do and start showing us that you are already doing it. You do *that* and not only would we come to your church, we'd volunteer to help you accomplish those tasks.

We are tired of the same old unfulfilled promises, political pageantry and religious rhetoric. But that doesn't mean we don't want to help. It just means until you show us what you're doing instead of telling us what to do, we don't believe working with you is the answer.

Trust me, we don't need a miracle ... Just a reason to believe one could happen.

-Richard / Detroit, MI

Progress, Not Perfection

You don't have to win the race,
but you do need to finish it

As I sat there watching *Wheel of Fortune* on the small TV screen, my mother stepped out of the room to make a call and left me all alone ... just me. Well, Grandma was there, too – but she was asleep, her hospital bed causing her to sit awkwardly while an IV pumped something into her body that I can only assume numbs her pain. As a 37-year-old man, I had never seen my grandmother in such a state and I'd certainly never been totally alone with her – at least not like this.

For the first time since I was a little boy, I felt scared.

My grandmother had been diagnosed with cancer at 84 years of age, and we weren't really sure if she was going to make it. Being in my 30s, and one of 18 grandchildren, I felt unworthy of my current position. "What if she dies now?" I thought to myself, "Here? With no one else in the room but me? I'm not supposed to be the last one she sees."

After a few minutes, my mother returned and asked if I'd mind staying alone with Grandma a little longer while she went to get us some food. I obliged, uncomfortably, but didn't show it. I wanted to remain strong for her, so she could be strong for my grandmother.

After hours of being asleep, and nearly 30 minutes after my mother's departure, Grandma began to wake up. My worst fear was happening. I began to panic. "What should I say?" I thought. "What *can* I say? The woman is 84 years old. What am I going to say to her she hasn't already heard?" I felt helpless.

"Matthew," she said in a slow, breathy voice, "come closer."

"Yes ma'am," I said, moving my chair up against her bed. As I did, she squeezed my hand so tightly that my fingers began to go numb.

"I should've laughed more. I should've smiled more. I should've had more fun," she told me. "I shouldn't have taken life so seriously."

I struggled to swallow. *"Oh my God ... this is it. She's about to die right now,"* I remember thinking. *"Please God, not now. Not with only me here."*

"You have your whole life ahead of you," she said as she interrupted my thoughts. "You still have time ... time to change, time to laugh, time to live ...

Don't waste it."

Right at that moment the hospital door opened wide and in walked my mother with our food. "Oh, is she awake?" she asked, putting the food down and walking toward the bed. I started to reply, but when I turned back to my grandmother, I saw she had already fallen back to sleep. I didn't tell my mother what Grandma said to me. I didn't know if I should.

Two days later, my grandmother passed. She never woke up after that last conversation with me. I was the last one to ever hear her speak. *And I didn't like that.* I felt ashamed, like I had stolen that moment away from my mother. She should've been the one to hear my grandmother's last words, not me.

At the funeral, my mother sang my grandmother's favorite song, "Where the Roses Never Fade." As she did, she began to cry. She managed to finish the song (barely) and motioned for me to come up and say a few words while she composed herself. This was *not*

122

part of the plan and I was not prepared. "Oh God," I thought to myself, "it's like the hospital room all over again." I hesitated before rising and felt my mouth getting dry. I had no idea what to say. And then suddenly, as I looked out at all those in attendance who were waiting to hear some inspiring story or word of wisdom, it all became so clear …

" 'I should've laughed more. I should've smiled more. I should've had more fun. I shouldn't have taken life so seriously.' These are the last words my grandmother ever spoke to me."

I then reached over to my mother and squeezed her hand, as I sternly spoke …

" 'You,' Grandma told me, 'You have your whole life ahead of you. You still have time … time to change, time to laugh, time to live … Don't waste it.' "

And with that, I sat down. Held back my tears. And vowed to keep my grandmother's wishes.

-Matthew / Buffalo, NY

***UPDATE: It's been three years since I shared that story. I wish I could end it right there and say that all has gone well. You know, that I've followed my grandmother's advice – laughing and living more. It'd make for a great story, I'm sure. But the truth is, I haven't led the life she wished for me. As a matter of fact, I haven't even come close.

Let me explain …

About a year after my grandmother passed, my wife Danielle and I separated. Why? I made some poor financial decisions against her better judgment that put our family's lifestyle in jeopardy. It was such a strain on us financially (not to mention embarrassing to me) that she filed for a legal separation. I came home one day to find that she and the kids – Andy, 11, and Emily, 9 – had packed their things and moved out. I was shocked. It was hard enough when my grandmother was taken from me, but Grandma had no choice in the matter, she died. My wife and kids? They were alive and well … and living 10 minutes away in a small apartment across town. *They chose to leave.*

To add insult to injury, during this time I barely saw my kids. How could I? "Our kids" were technically my wife's kids – from a previous marriage – so naturally they left with her when she moved out. Me having raised them since they were 4 and 2, and basically being the only father they'd ever known, you can imagine how devastating that was for me (and them).

I absolutely hated it.

To make matters worse, three months after of our separation, I lost my job. Although it wasn't my fault – my company decided to downsize – it sure didn't help me improve things with Danielle. There I was trying to regain her trust and show her I could be the provider I once was, and now my only source of income was gone.

Out of work, I had no choice but to file for unemployment.

With no way to support my family, and no family to come home to, I fell into a deep depression. Within a month I started smoking … again. Eight years without a single cigarette and suddenly I had one in my hand every hour. I was losing control of my life and I knew it. Something had to change.

Which leads us to where I am now …

This past year has been a whirlwind of events. Although I've had plenty of ups and downs, I gotta say, things are finally getting better.

Did Danielle and kids move back home? No. At least not yet. But she and I *did* manage to avoid a divorce and we have started going to counseling. If things continue as they are, I think she and the kids will move back within the next month or two. So there's still hope.

Did I find full-time employment? Kind of. The company I used to work for was bought by a local competitor and they recently hired me to take on a two-year project with them. It may not be a long-term, permanent position, but it's a start. And the money I make now is better than anything I made before, so I am happy to accept.

Did I stop smoking? No. But I *have* cut back and plan to cut it out entirely very soon. (Our marriage counselor always says, "One thing at a time," and I couldn't agree more. When I'm ready, I will. If I did it before, I know I can do it again.)

So as you can see, I certainly do not have a perfect ending to this story. Not by any means. And I am far from crossing my Finish Line in the race to get my life back together. But things *are* getting better.

So what changed?

I did.

I decided if I want a better life, I should start with being a better father and husband. So I apologized to Danielle for all the pain I've caused her and the kids and told her if she'd give me another chance, I would show her the husband and father I can be, instead of the self-centered man I've been.

I also decided to get honest with myself. I understand that I am a work-in-progress. I realize that I have a lot of faults and they're not all going to be solved overnight – and I'm okay with that.

I don't have to come in First Place. I don't have to be number one. I just have to finish – finish what I've started and do the best I can, when I can. (And thank God that's all I have to do, because honestly, right now it's all I *can* do.)

Despite my recent actions, if my grandmother were here today, I believe she'd be even more proud of me now than ever before. Not because I'm laughing more, living more or making the most of my time. But because despite all my failures, *I still believe I can* – a belief given to me while she lay dying, in hopes that I might live.

-Matthew / Buffalo, NY

(Un)Lucky In Love

To strike out, one must be unlucky three times.
To hit a home run, one must be lucky only once

Sometimes people we love don't care that we do.
Sometimes people we love don't love us back.
Sometimes people we love don't even know we do.
Sometimes people we love hurt us worse than they hurt others.
Sometimes people we love love someone else.

Sometimes people we love stop loving us.
Sometimes people we love are the ones we wish we didn't.
Sometimes people we love leave.
Sometimes people we love control us.
Sometimes people we love lie and cheat.

Sometimes people we love change.
Sometimes people we love forget the good but remember the bad.
Sometimes people we love are toxic.
Sometimes people we love aren't worth it.
Sometimes people we love hate us.

However ...

Sometimes people we love are the most caring people we know.
Sometimes people we love love us more than we love ourselves.
Sometimes people we love show us love every day.
Sometimes people we love heal us.
Sometimes people we love love us more than anyone else.

Sometimes people we love love us beyond the grave.
Sometimes people we love are a wish come true.
Sometimes people we love stay when others leave.
Sometimes people we love help us take control.
Sometimes people we love defend us.

Sometimes people we love grow with us.
Sometimes people we love bring out the best in us.
Sometimes people we love make our lives better.
Sometimes people we love are priceless.
Sometimes people we love are *in love* with us.

Therefore ...

The question is, "Is love worth the risk?"

Well, let me put it to you this way: If I were a gambling man, I'd never bet more money than I could afford to lose. If I were winning, I'd keep playing. If I started losing, I'd slow down. And if my losing streak continued, I'd stop ... long before my funds were depleted.

Love isn't risky. *People are.*

Find the right people and you can bet on them every time.

-MJ Wilson

Why Is My Personal Trainer In Worse Shape Than I Am?

Don't judge a bird by its color

Okay ... so after two years of constant nagging from my wife, I finally broke down and decided to join a gym. Since I'm almost 40 years old and haven't touched a barbell since high school, I figured I should start out with a personal trainer. I told my wife, "The last thing I want to do is injure myself while trying to become healthier." She actually believed me. (The truth was, I was embarrassed to try to work all those new machines without any help. I didn't want to look stupid.) Before I began, I also decided to get a physical from my doctor. Maybe I was overdoing it, but besides being embarrassed about working out, I didn't want to risk doing anything stupid.

My physician told me three very important things to remember. One: the weight range I should be in, given my height and build. (Apparently I need to lose 20-25 lbs.) Two: the types of foods I should and should not be eating (you know ... more fruits and vegetables, less junk food, blah blah blah). And three – I needed to exercise for at least 30 minutes a day, three times per week. (Now I was actually kind of excited about that one because I knew I could meet that goal.)

My first night at the gym I arrived to meet Joe, my trainer. As I was sitting in one of those comfy chairs (you know the kind – they look like they belong in a fancy furniture store) waiting to begin, around the corner came a guy about the same height as me (5'10") and nearly the same age (maybe five or six years younger), but as far as his weight ... Ohhhh myyyyy ... The guy looked like he was gonna explode out of his official "Personal Trainer" t-shirt. He was huge – *and not in a good way.* His belly was so far over his belt he couldn't tuck his shirt in if he wanted to! Trust me, if I was 25 lbs overweight, this guy had to *easily* be 60-70 lbs overweight, if not more! His pants were so tight and his shirt was so small, it actually looked comical.

I knew there was nooo waaay this was for real ... it had to be a joke. I mean, gyms don't hire overweight people as personal trainers ... right?

In our 14 years of marriage, my wife and I have always played little tricks on each other. And since my 40th birthday was next month, I figured this was just another gag she conjured up, to dog me for taking so long to get back in shape. I felt sure I was on camera somewhere and she was probably watching, and whatever I did in the next few minutes was probably gonna be viewed at my party by all our friends and family. So what did I do?

I laughed. *A lot.*

So much that my eyes watered and my stomach actually started to hurt. I couldn't help it ... I couldn't hold it in any longer. I laughed and cried and thanked "Joe" (if that was his real name) for playing along and then I looked around and shouted, "Okay Heather, you can come out now. You got me. Joke's over."

Joe just stared at me. He had no idea what was going on. With a polite, but concerned tone, he said to me, "Are you all right, sir? Is there something I don't know about?"

I looked at him while trying to calm down and catch my breath and said, "Okay Joe" (I even made the little quotes gesture with my fingers as I said his name), "it's cool. You got me. Obviously you're not a *real* trainer, but that's okay. I appreciate the joke. Now where's my wife? Where's the camera?"

Joe said nothing.

Heather was nowhere to be found.

Uh-oh. Joe *was* a real trainer.

And I looked like a total a**hole.

Feeling horrible, I apologized profusely. I was so embarrassed. And although Joe was still willing to keep our appointment, I told him I wanted to reschedule for another time. I couldn't go through with it after what I had just done. I suppose he agreed ... I don't really know. I left before he could even answer. I just wanted to get out of there.

Three days later, I got a call at home. It was Joe. He asked me to meet with him privately at a local bar so we could talk. He said he wanted to share something with me about the gym. It sounded a little strange to me, but feeling guilty for what I had already done, I agreed.

When we met, Joe told me about his life-long dream of being a bodybuilder and personal trainer (which started making me feel even worse). He even pulled out a few photos of himself from just a few years prior when he used to compete and was first hired at the gym. He looked amazing. Totally different than the Joe I was looking at now. I couldn't believe how much he had changed. And I didn't know why he was showing me all of this. I felt bad enough already.

"If you don't mind me asking," I said, "what happened?"

"My mother died. Brain tumor. We never saw it coming. She was only 52."

Talk about going from bad to worse. "I'm so sorry." I said. "I can't imagine how hard that must've been."

"She was the only one who truly believed in me. The only one who believed I could make it. When she died, it was like all the hope and motivation I had died with her. I just gave up."

At this point I'm feeling 10 times worse than I did at the gym. I remember thinking, "Where is this guy going with this?"

"I fell into a deep depression," he said. "I started eating and basically never stopped. Now here I am three years later and 80 pounds heavier, trying to get back on track."

I didn't know what to say. I just sat there in disbelief and feeling like such a jerk. And then he drops this on me ...

"They fired me ... the gym, that is. They let me go. My manager heard about what happened between you and me and told me I was 'bad for business.' Said I could come back when I 'get my act together.'"

As I began to apologize again, he interrupted me and said, "No ... you don't get it. I'm *glad* this happened. Your response when you saw me for the first time – it's what people have thought all along but never had the guts to say. It's what I needed to hear. It's inspired me to become the man I've always wanted to be. The man my mother always believed I could be. I'm through with being 'Big Joe' – overweight and out of shape. I'm ready to take my life back. I'm ready to make that change."

I was impressed (and relieved, too) and told him I was happy for his decision. I told him I was sure his mother would be proud.

"I'm not done," he said. "I've already joined the smaller gym just down the road. Nobody knows me there. I'm gonna start all over and I want you to start with me. I need a workout partner ... someone to keep me motivated ... someone to be real and honest with me ... that's definitely you," he said with a smile. "And besides, you need a trainer ... someone to help you work out ... someone who knows what they're doing. Just look at my pictures. If I looked like that before, I can look like that again. And I can take you on the same journey with me. We can both do this."

I thought about his proposal. It sounded tempting. He interrupted my thinking.

"C'mon! I help you, you help me. Besides, all my services will be free. I just need someone who'll keep me honest. Keep us real. Whattaya say?"

How could I not agree to that? I'm getting a free personal trainer and a workout partner. What else could I ask for?

"Sure," I said. "Let's do it. I've got nothin' to lose but weight anyway, right? Besides, I know me … If I don't have someone to keep me accountable, I'll never stick with it. "

"Then it's settled," he said. "Meet me there this Monday at 5 p.m. and we'll get started."

And I did.

Six months later, here I am … 25 lbs lighter (my target weight) and maintaining. And Joe? He's down 50 lbs and more determined than ever. It's been a great journey.

If I've learned anything from this unlikely friendship, it's this: It's not what you did that matters (that's your past and there's nothing you can do about it). It's what you do *after* what you did. That's what counts.

Everyone messes up, but not everyone cleans up.

Joe and I … we cleaned up.

-Brian / Bloomington, IN

What Doesn't Kill You, *Tried To*

(Do you really need a subtitle for this one? The title alone should be enough to make you think twice.)

Some time ago, as I was cleaning my kitchen waiting for *The Wendy Williams Show* to come on TV so I could get my daily fix of "Hot Topics" (I just *love* watching her show), a female guest on another TV show (you know the kind ... the "Baby Mama-Drama" type), shouted one of the most perplexing statements I've ever heard.

"He says he's only cheated on me six times, but I KNOW he's cheated eight! And I'M GONNA PROVE IT TODAY!"

If you could see the face I made when those words entered my ears. (Picture a dog staring at you, then slowly tilting its head to one side.) Did I just hear that right? He cheated six times but she wants to prove it was eight? Huh???

I just *had* to hear the rest of the story. (I know ... that's a lame excuse, but it's the truth!) I put down the dishrag, took off my cleaning gloves and sat in front of the TV.

Short version of the story: The accused lover, after several bleeped curse words, endless denials, and seemingly a million "Baby you know I love you ... I'd never cheat on you *that* many times," were pleaded, the official lie-detector results were in. And wouldn't you know it? He *hadn't* cheated on her eight times. He had cheated more than 16 times! And as bad as this may sound, this isn't the part that has me the most confused.

Upon hearing the results of the lie-detector test, you would think the victim – the young lady who was cheated on – would be devastated, right? Emotionally distraught, perhaps crying uncontrollably or even running off the stage in disgust. But no, not this girl. What did she do? (Are you ready for this? You won't believe it.)

The young lady jumped up and down, swooping her fist in the air (as in victorious celebration) yelling over and over, "I TOLD YOU I WAS RIGHT! I KNEW YOU WERE LYING! I KNEW IT!!!"

Apparently the consolation of proving him to have cheated more than six times on her was greater than the fact that … um … gee … I don't know … he cheated on her MORE THAN 16 TIMES!

(Surely I'm not the only one who sees the madness in this, right?)

After watching this, I couldn't help but think about the rest of us. I mean sure, I know most of us aren't naïve enough (or some may even say, "stupid enough") to stay with a lover like that, thinking that person will change and be faithful. But how many of us continue to remain faithful to a company, a belief, a job, cause, friend, or, in some cases, maybe we *have* stayed with a lover, which if we were honest with ourselves has treated us no better?

Think of it this way: How many times does a lover have to cheat on you before he or she is no longer a lover, but rather, a cheater? Five times? Ten times? Is there really a difference between her lover cheating 16 times and yours cheating four?

Or what about your job? How many years should you remain faithful to a company that's constantly been unfaithful to you, giving promised promotions to someone else or always doing you wrong? When is enough, enough?

It reminds me of a joke I was told some years ago. An older gentleman enters a bar and sees a young, beautiful girl. He walks up to her and asks if she would be willing to have sex with him.

She looks at him in disgust and says, "Absolutely not!" To which he replies, "How about if I pay you $1000?" She then says, "Hmmm ... a thousand dollars? Sure. Why not?"

As she picks up her coat and purse and prepares to leave with him, the older gentleman asks her one last question: "I know we agreed on a thousand, but I was wondering, would you be willing to have sex with me for $100 instead?"

Immediately the girl becomes infuriated and shouts, "HEY! WHAT KIND OF GIRL DO YOU THINK I AM?" To which he replies, "I think we've already established that. Now I'm just trying to get a discount."

The point I'm trying to make is, we too often sell ourselves short in life.

Are we like the girl in the joke who has been bought off with a few extra dollars to be something we really don't want to be? Or look at the lady with the lover who cheated 16 times. She won her argument. But what did that "win" get her? A lousy lover and bragging rights? Seriously?

I've heard people say many, many times, "What doesn't kill you only makes you stronger." But I've always thought, "Yeah, maybe that's true. But you're missing the point. Whatever it was that tried to kill you, *tried to kill you*."

Just because you beat it, it doesn't mean it was worth what it took to do so.

Some battles are better off not fought. Not that you should put up with stuff ... on the contrary, *don't put up with stuff at all*.

Walk away.
Quit.
Leave.
Get out.
Cancel.
Move on.

Do whatever you have got to do to get past it. And once you've moved on, use your newly found time and energy on battles worth the risk and the reward.

I realize you can't do this with everything, and that's okay ... that's life. But if you're honest with yourself, you'll see you can do this with a lot more stuff in your life than you think. And your life could be a lot less cluttered and stressful than it is right now.

Remember, sometimes a win is a loss in disguise. Believe me.

Life's too short to be competing for a trophy that's worth less than the entrance fee you paid to enter the competition in the first place.

-MJ Wilson

More Responsibility, Same Pay. Wait ... What?

You don't have to know where you're going
to know you need to leave where you are

After working as a top seller of women's clothing for six years, my company (a major retail store that I'll keep anonymous) decides I have what it takes to manage my own department and offers me a position as a manager.

Now normally this would be a welcomed invitation. I mean, after more than half a decade of working long shifts (typically standing the entire time while helping customers), suffering fluctuating schedules and paychecks (some weeks I got 40 hours of work, other weeks I got as little as 17), and making only minimum wage + a small commission (which has never been enough to live on), you'd think an offer like this would be great, right?

No longer would I be at the mercy of my boss if I suddenly needed a day off. No more wondering what my schedule would be or how many hours I would get. No more small checks or lack of health benefits. And beyond all that, no more answering to the boss!

I WOULD be the boss! Who wouldn't want that? This was finally a chance for me to really make an improvement in my life.

My immediate supervisor and our store manager ask to meet with me during my lunch break to discuss the details. According to the offer, the first 90 days would be a probationary period, during which I'd qualify for no health benefits, no commission eligibility (if I happened to make any sales of my own) and have no real "power" (all major decisions would be made by another "mentoring manager" while I observed and learned).

At the end of the 90-day period, if my mentoring manager approved my managing skills and felt I was ready to take over, he would then recommend to the higher-ups that I manage my own department. If not, back to the sales floor I go.

Now this might sound reasonable to you, but what you don't understand is this offer was made to me in late October. They wanted my probationary period to start mid-November (the week before Thanksgiving) and end sometime around Valentine's Day. They offered to pay me a bi-weekly salary based upon my average sales per hour plus my commission for the previous three months.

Do you see the problem with this? They want me to work for them during our *busiest* season of the entire year with no chance to make any extra money. In other words, they want to pay me a salary based upon my SLOWEST sales time of the year and save themselves money by NOT paying me my average sales during our major holiday season (especially during "Black Friday" or Christmas), aka MY BEST sales time of the year!

To make matters worse, because I would now be a manager (at least on paper), my weekly schedule would be anywhere from 50-60 hours (or more) per week (at least during the holiday season, which is practically my entire probationary period), oftentimes working from open to close! All this while making a salary and NOT an hourly wage, so no matter how many hours I work per week I still get paid only for a 40-hour work week.

Why would I want to do this???

As I sit and listen to their "exciting news" (as they put it), I begin to think just what a crock of sh*t all of this really is and wonder how they can sit there across the table from me with a straight face and act like they're doing me a favor. Do I really look *that* stupid? Who do they think I am? Before I could voice my opinion or offer any reply at all, one of them actually said to me, "This could be your big chance to move up the corporate ladder ... A once-in-a-lifetime opportunity. So whattaya think? Do you want it?"

At this point I'm thinking, "Do I want it? Are you outta your mind? HELL NO I don't want this!" But trying to control myself so as not to cause problems, I said what everyone says when they get offers like this ... "Can I think about it and get back to you in a day or two?" To which they agreed and our meeting was done.

The next day, while sitting in the break room at work discussing my "exciting news" with a few of my co-workers, one of them reminded me about my first day on the job.

"Angie ... I remember the day you got hired. I introduced myself and told you I had been here for five years already and would be happy to help you with anything you may need. Do you remember that? 'Cause I do. And I remember your reply ... *'This is not a career move for me, it's only a job. If I'm still here five years from now, shoot me ... please.'* Do you remember that? Huh, Ang? What happened to that? You want me to shoot you now?" And then he chuckled and said, "You'll be here the rest of your life, just like the rest of us."

Whatever he said after that I have no idea. It was like everything went blurry and I began to have an out-of-body experience. I saw myself 25 years in the future either still begging my boss for a day off, standing in heels all day worn out from getting short breaks and no time to sit, wondering if I'd get 20, 30 or 40 hours on the schedule next week, tired, stressed and sick of it all OR working 50-60 hours a week as a manager, making a minimal salary, stressed over sales quotas.

Either way I was screwed.

I re-entered the present from my epiphany to find my co-workers still chuckling at my fate – our fate – and told them the following:

"You are exactly right ... I will be here the rest of my life. Just like all of you ... unless I do something about it." I then stood up and started walking towards the time clock where we punch in and out for work. It was only 10 feet away, but the walk seemed like something out of a movie in slow motion. With every step, I noticed my co-workers looking up at me, and then one of them said, "What are you gonna do, Ang? Where are you going?"

As I arrived in front of the clock, I pulled out my timecard, held it up to the machine and paused. I looked over at my co-workers one last time. Leon, the one who had reminded me of my fate to begin with, stood up and said, "Don't do it Angie ... You'll regret it." To which I looked at him with a questionable stare that slowly turned into a grim smile and said, "The only thing I regret is staying here as long as I have." Then I swiped my card and walked out, while they all watched in disbelief.

That was nearly six years ago.

So where am I now? I went back to school. I graduated and now I'm an admissions counselor at a local college and advisor for several students each year. I help them decide what they want to do for a career and help them find the best course of action to make it happen so they don't end up in a job they regret the rest of their lives.

Imagine that.

-Angie / Cleveland, OH

If It Ain't Workin', It Ain't Workin'

*Whatever you do in life, someone will love it,
someone will hate it, and most won't care.*

The bright green, over-sized digital numbers on my clock tell me it's 3 a.m. I'm half awake, sitting on the edge of my bed alongside Kristin, my best friend, listening to her go on and on about how messed up her life is ... why she's unhappy with her boyfriend (dating for three years now and still no ring); her job (six years with a stellar sales career and still no promotion); and her family (her parents are still angry that she didn't want to work for the family business and they refuse to have anything to do with her, despite her attempts to make peace).

Apparently nothing in her life seems to be working right, and I'm the lucky one to share her pain. Now I don't wanna sound like a b*tch (really, I don't), but she's told me this story a million times before, and as much as I love her, *I gotta get some sleep*. Work comes early for me. So, as her swollen, watery eyes and tightly clenched tissues paint the saddest scene you could ever imagine, I look over at her and gently say, "I'm sorry but I gotta go to bed. It's really late."

"But wait," she says. "I know I normally tell you I just wanna vent, but tonight's different. I can't take this anymore. I'm sick of feeling this way. Please tell me what you think I should do."

Now at this point I'm so tired I don't want to answer that question. But this is the first time she's actually asked me for my advice and

141

there is no *waaaay* I'm gonna miss this opportunity. So I stand up, put on my glasses, and tell her the following story from my teenage years:

"It was the summer after my 7th-grade year. My boyfriend Travis and I were waiting in line at the Krasher Kars bumper car ride, just dying for the operator to lift the gate and let us in. When he did, we blew past him, both of us making a beeline towards the car we thought was best. I quickly found mine – a blue-and-white racer with a faded number seven on the side – and jumped inside. I put on the seatbelt and waited. My heart was racing. I knew in a matter of seconds I would be ramming my car into Travis's repeatedly, while doing my best to avoid his and all others at the same time. Childish and silly? Sure. But what more could a 13-year-old girl who's crazy in love want?

Life was fun.

My life was fun.

I was happy."

Kristin lets out a deep sigh as she readjusts herself on my bed. She seems a little unsure of what to do with my advice so far, but is intently listening (which is rare for her), so I continue.

"'Three … Two … One … KRASH!' yelled the ride operator, and right when I heard the "kra" of "krash" I slammed my foot onto that gas pedal and white-knuckled the steering wheel. I had executed the perfect start except for one slight problem …

My car didn't budge. Not an inch.

Nothin'. Nada. Zilch.

It was like I was on TV and the joke was on me. You know, like one of those hidden camera shows.

Everyone else's car started right on cue, and their four minutes of inflicting terror had begun. I knew right then the longer I stayed where I was, the worse things were gonna get. I had to do something and do it fast or I was gonna get drilled about a zillion times – and I wasn't about to let that happen. I immediately took off my seatbelt, jumped out of my car (much to the dismay of the ride operator) and ran across the track towards the green car in the corner. Meanwhile, the ride operator was yelling at me, 'Please stay seated in your car until the ride is over!'

Stay seated? Are you CRAZY? Who does that??? The entire point of being in a bumper car is to BUMP INTO PEOPLE, not sit and watch 'em pass you by, let alone getting crushed yourself. I just acted like I didn't hear him and kept going. I was a girl on a mission and nothing was gonna stop me.

I jumped into the green car, slapped on my seatbelt and punched the gas. It took off immediately and I was back on track. More important, Travis was in sight and I was headed his way.

Life was fun.

My life was fun.

I was happy … *again.*

The End."

I look at Kristin. She scratches her head, squints her eyes and sincerely questions me.

"Um, why exactly did you just tell me that story? I don't see your point."

"To help you," I reply.

Now I imagine *you* understand why I told the story, but please allow me to share with you the explanation I gave to her:

"When we were young, we tended to be much more genuine with our feelings and much more honest with ourselves. If we liked something, we pursued it, captured it and kept it. We knew what we wanted and did whatever it took to get it. If we didn't like something, we got rid of it, let go of it or simply never latched on to it in the first place. Basically, if it didn't feel good, we weren't interested. (Yes, we may have been immature and naïve, but we at least knew what we wanted and weren't afraid to go after it.)

For some reason, although this logic worked for us 80-90 percent of the time, as we've gotten older, we've learned to hide our feelings, compromise our desires, settle for less than what we want or just accept whatever life gives us. Our ability to say yes or no to whomever or whatever, seemed to go out the window the minute we realized we might offend people or hurt their feelings if we don't do what everyone else thinks we should do.

It never dawns on us that in the long run, the only person who is truly being hurt and offended is ourselves. To make matters worse, we then repeat this process year after year until we become so numb to our pain we don't even realize just how "effed up" and backwards our life actually is.

The bumper car story? Well, it shows who we *used* to be.

Our brashness, our bareness, our rawness. When I was that little 13-year-old girl, I knew who I wanted (Travis), I knew what I wanted (bumper car number seven), and I knew what I wanted to do with it (ram it into Travis's car as many times as possible)."

I pause to take a drink from my water bottle sitting on top of my dresser. Kristin looks up at me to see why I stopped. She doesn't say a word. She's obviously expecting more and patiently waits. I wipe my mouth, put the cap back on the bottle and continue.

"When my car didn't budge, did I sit there and question its ability to work?"

Kristin glances over at me to see if I expect her to actually answer. When she realizes I'm waiting for a response, she shakes her head no, slowly.

"Did I complain about it and cry while simultaneously getting destroyed by other cars?"

I wait.

"No," she says, replying quicker this time, but seemingly a little annoyed I'm asking such an "elementary" question.

"Did I wait for someone to tell me to get out of it and find a better one?"

"NO," she says a little louder, slightly annoyed.

"And finally, did I listen to what others around me were telling me to do – stay seated in the car until the ride was over?"

This time I answer the question before she even has a chance to reply.

"*HELL NO!*

I took my problems into my own hands. And I kept life simple."

Now before I go any further I've got to stop right here because I know what some of you are thinking … "Jasmine, you didn't keep life simple. *It was already simple.* Bumper cars are not the same as relationships or jobs or family matters. You were a teenager. Adulthood is much more serious and complex."

And my reply to you is, "But that's because we have a perspective of what life is currently like for us, where teens don't. We forget that, in the moment of being a teenager, life WAS complex. We were dealing with new situations all the time – dating, friendships, parents, school, our changing bodies, etc. Life was tough. Yet in the middle of all that confusion and complexity, we still knew what we liked and didn't like and acted accordingly. (Think clothing styles, teachers, music, sports, etc. and I think you'll agree.)

Good or bad, if we weren't feelin' it, we moved on from it.

And as for adulthood being complex … well, that's debatable as well. Sure, we have more responsibilities and greater expectations, but we also have more freedoms available to us and more control over what we do. Just because it's more complex doesn't mean it has to be more confusing.

Anyway, let's get back to Kristen and me ...

The bright green, over-sized digital numbers on my clock now tell me it's 3:33 a.m. I'm really tired and feeling drained. I need to get to bed, but I can't leave Kristin hanging. So I become even more direct:

"Girl, if you're not happy with your boyfriend, I don't care how long you two have dated, how many memories you've shared, or how many people think you make a great couple. If it ain't workin', it ain't workin'. You'd better get out and get out now ... while you can. Believe me, it's better to be single than to wish you were. Especially when there are kids and finances involved."

By this time Kristin is gripping both pillows intensely on her lap while staring at the floor. She just sits there in silence.

"And your job?" I question. "The last thing you want to do is sit there and do nothing, and then expect things to just magically improve. If you'll recall, I didn't wait for the ride operator to tell me it was okay to leave my car – he actually tried to get me to stay! I got up and did what I had to do to take care of ME! You're gonna have to do the same.

I'm tellin' you ... If your boss hasn't promoted you yet, I highly doubt she ever will."

Kristin, now wiping her tears, exhales another long, tiresome sigh.

"And as for your family ... That's even easier. Baby you have to live for yourself and no one else. It's not their place to judge you. If you've done all you can to make peace with them and they're not interested, then I say peace out and keep it movin'. Apologizing to them over and over would be like me constantly stepping on the gas pedal in that bumper car and thinking eventually it's just gonna work. Not only is it a waste of time ... it's foolish."

"Okay Jasmine! You've made your point. I get it," she says, reaching for the box of tissues next to my water.

I stop, sit down, put my arm around her and give her a big hug. After a minute or two, she tells me thanks, says she's got some thinking to do and then sees her way out. I turn out the lights and go to bed. I'm exhausted.

Kristen … Will she do the right thing? I don't know. Only time will tell. But one thing I DO know – Whatever she does or you do in life, someone will love it, someone will hate it, and most won't care. So she and you might as well do what you want. Make your own decisions, enjoy life while you can and remember these three things:

1) It's okay to expect to be happy.
2) It's okay to expect to be happy.
3) It's okay to expect to be happy.

Are you getting the picture?

Listen, I know life isn't always great – we all go through something now and then. But that's just it … WE GO THROUGH IT – WE DON'T STAY THERE. You gotta keep things moving or you'll fall into a pit of depression that's nearly impossible to get out of. Believe me, I've seen it happen many times … Beautiful people who once had such bright spirits give in and give up, only to become dark, depressed and lonely. It's so sad.

It really is okay to expect to be happy in life … *your life*. And it's okay to want more. Just know you may need to let go of some people or positions.

Once this happens, I believe you will see …

Life will be fun.

Your life will be fun.

And you'll be happy … *again*.

-*Jasmine / New Orleans, LA*

Well ... *Look Who's Talking*

Reality has less to do with what's real,
and more to do with who's realizing it

You decided a high school diploma was enough. I earned a college degree. **You** stopped your education. I kept going.

You decided the gym just wasn't for you. I lost 30 pounds. **You** stopped working out. I still go three times a week.

You settled for the first man that wanted a family. I waited for the man I wanted a family *with*. **You**'re getting a divorce. I'm getting a second honeymoon.

You took a second mortgage to pay for **you**r new car. I took money from my savings to buy a used one. **You**r car was repossessed. Mine was repainted.

Your house is a mess. My house is my home. **You** don't clean **you**rs anymore. I don't let mine get dirty.

Your kids don't obey **you**. Mine don't wanna let me down. **You** gave up on disciplining your kids. *I gave up on expecting others to raise mine.*

Your co-workers annoy **you**. I love what I do. **You** have a job. I have a career.

You don't like me anymore. I still love **you** with all my heart. **You** think I'm lucky. I think **you**'re hurting.

Do I think I'm better than **you**? Of course not. Do I deserve to be happier? Not at all. But one thing **you** need to realize … **YOU** were the one that made **you**r decisions, not me. **You** chose to stop when I chose to keep going.

I refuse to apologize for reaching my goals and living my dream just because I worked a little harder or expected a little more out of life and myself. I am not sorry.

But make no mistake about it … I DO NOT think I'm better than **you**. That would be <u>ridiculous</u>. I just think I believed *we could* at a time in our lives when **you** believed we couldn't. And *that* has made all the difference.

-The Possible You / Anywhere, U.S.A.

A Lesbian, Atheist And Church Girl Walk Into A Bar

Until we try, possibilities are merely ... possibilities

There I was, nearly five months into my freshman year and still no friends. Well ... no *close* friends. Coming from a small town in Alabama and not one to travel much, I wasn't exactly the outgoing type. (If it weren't for my family's annual trip to my aunt's house here in Atlanta each Christmas, I don't think I would've ever had the courage to attend college here. At the time, Atlanta was just too far away and too big for me. I was definitely a "Daddy's girl.")

Growing up, I was home-schooled by my mother and lived within walking distance of the only church I'd attended my entire life. I pretty much existed from sun up to sun down within a five-mile radius of my home. This made for a simple life, sure, but for a sheltered one, too – although I didn't know it at the time.

Making friends didn't exactly come easy for me ... but Stephanie changed all of that.

Me being only 19, Stephanie – a 22-year-old junior transfer from a neighboring school and the oldest of my three suitemates – was like the older sister I'd never had. She was funny, very out-spoken, and definitely a city girl. Between our uncommon interests (I was fascinated by how much she knew about life, she was fascinated by how much I *didn't*), and her sense of humor, we really hit it off.

We became friends – close friends – very fast.

Which brings me to the story I want to share with you now - The time our lives and friendship changed … for the better.

One weekend, Stephanie sends me a text wanting me to meet her at a bar near her old campus after she gets off work. She says her buddy John from high school will be joining us. I tell her I'm happy to, but I don't know John and I've never been in a bar before, so I'm a little uncomfortable. She texts back, "Welcome to college life, sweetie!" And that's that. Next thing you know, I'm sitting at a table in a dark corner, nervously waiting for Stephanie and John to arrive, while praying to God my parents never find out I'm in a bar!

After 10 minutes or so, I get a text from Stephanie letting me know that she's running late, but that John will be arriving any minute. (She sent him a pic of me so he'd know what I look like.) According to Stephanie's texts, "He's the tall, dark and handsome type. You'll know him when you see him."

Well let me tell you, she wasn't lying! About a minute later, John – over 6 feet tall, black hair, blue eyes – strolls in and walks right up to me.

"Hi, I'm John. It's nice to meet you."

Immediately I think, "For a guy this hot, Stephanie sure doesn't talk about him much. She's been holding out on me."

"It's nice to meet you, too," I reply. "I'm Jennifer. So glad you could make it."

"Sorry I'm late," he says. "My car is in the shop, so I had a friend of mine drop me off. I'll just catch a ride with Stephanie on the way home."

He then takes a seat, orders a beer and begins to tell me a story about how he and Stephanie met. Before he can finish, Stephanie arrives, plops down in between the two of us, takes a drink of his beer, and starts right in. (This is where the party really begins. Stephanie's funny *all the time*. Adding alcohol and John to the mix

151

only makes her more interesting.)

Before you know it, two hours have gone by and they're still going strong. They talk and drink and laugh … and drink some more. Although I'm tempted to try one of their drinks (and Stephanie orders one for me), I tell her I can't.

"You're going to need a designated driver, you know. Neither one of you are in any shape to drive home."

She and John both agree, and I'm off the hook … and relieved. (I keep having images of my father walking in while I've got a tall glass of beer in my hand. I can visualize him escorting me out by my ear in front of everyone while reminding me of how I was "raised better than that." That image alone is enough to keep me sober.)

Although I'm not intoxicated like Stephanie and John, it doesn't matter. I'm having a great time and enjoying the stories they're sharing about their high-school memories … Skipping school, cheating on exams, sneaking out at night to go on beer runs. Stuff I wouldn't dream of doing in a million years.

For the first time all year, I finally feel the way I do when I'm home. You know … safe. Protected. Having fun. So much fun, that the fact that I'm in a bar has totally escaped me. In this moment, it's just us. And I don't want it to stop.

"Would the two of you like to go home with me next weekend and meet my family?" I blurt out. "My church is having its homecoming picnic next Sunday and I'd love for you both to go. Besides, I really don't wanna make the three-hour drive by myself."

I'm a little embarrassed by what I've just asked, fearing they might make fun of me, but before I can retract my statement …

"Sure," says John. "I'd love to go."

"Me, too," says Stephanie, as she grabs my hand. "Sounds fun."

She then smiles at me, pulls me closer, and jokingly acts as if she's going to kiss me.

"You're drunk," I tell her, pulling my hand away and facing John.

"And you can't be acting this crazy when we go. You both gotta promise me you won't mention *anything* about alcohol or our trip to this bar, or ..."

"Oh relax," Stephanie interrupts. "There are bigger problems in the world ... like finding the restroom! I feel like I'm gonna pee my pants."

As she stands to leave, John gives her a quick smack on the butt and laughs as he sits back down.

Wanting to change the subject and get the focus off me, I turn to John.

"You really like her, don't you?"

"Me?" John replies, his eyes widening. "I think Stephanie's great. But YOU'RE the one she wants!"

"Huh? Whattaya mean by that?"

John continues without answering my question.

"Besides, I think the two of you would make a great couple."

He stops and takes a long, final swig of his beer. I just sit there, my head starting to swim, attempting to understand what he meant by his last statement. Before I can make any conclusion, he starts again ...

"And while I'm at it, I should probably tell you ... Although I really do want to go to your church's picnic, *I'm an atheist*. I just want you to know because although I don't have a problem with going, I know that some church folks are very critical of having an atheist in their service – let alone a lesbian."

(If this were a video, this is where you'd see tumbleweed going across the screen while the sound of a gentle wind blows through the air.)

OH.
MY.
GOSH.

Am I *that* blind? How could I not see it? Stephanie … a lesbian? *Wow.*

I feel embarrassed, naïve and stupid. I really don't know what to do, other than crawl under the table and hide. Forget the alcohol, I now have a lesbian and atheist coming to my church homecoming with me!

Unsure of what to say next, I quickly take a drink of my water, hoping to stall for time. It doesn't work, and I eventually have to answer.

"Of course," I almost whisper. "That's fine … It's no big deal."

But honestly, it IS a big deal! It's a HUGE deal!

What will my family say?
What will my church think?
What is happening to me?

As John pays the bar tab, back comes Stephanie and we all agree it's time to go. The ride home is rather quiet. John falls asleep in the back seat, as does Stephanie in the front.

I just sit.

And drive.

And think.

I now realize the world I've been living in – a small, sheltered bubble – is the world *I live in*. It's not necessarily everyone else's. And mine is changing … fast.

The following weekend, ready or not, here I am with the two of them, arriving at my church for the 10 a.m. service and picnic to follow. My parents are delightfully surprised. (I didn't tell them we were coming ... I didn't want to answer any more questions than necessary about John or Stephanie.) After a very brief introduction, we all take our seats just before the sermon begins.

"Oh God," I pray, "I know you are the only one who can truly judge another human being. *Please*, do me this one favor and let today's sermon be one that we all can agree upon."

About five seconds later, my pastor clips on his lapel mic and begins to speak.

"Can we all just get along?" he asks. "I mean really ... *Can we?* Is it actually possible? With so many different mindsets, beliefs, causes and concerns ... can we all *truly* get along?"

By this point, my heart is beating so hard in my chest I feel like John and Stephanie can hear it. Where is my pastor going with this? What's he gonna say next? *God what are you doing to me???*

"Well let me put it to you this way," he continues. "Oil and water don't mix, but you *can* hold them both in the same container. Now keep in mind when you do, they literally will not mix," he says, as he raises a glass full of water and begins pouring in oil, "yet they CAN remain peaceably side by side, without giving up their properties ... Something to consider."

I let out a deep sigh of relief. My heartbeat begins to slow down.

Looks like I'm gonna be okay.

The rest of the sermon and the church picnic go just as I had hoped – full of memories with good food and great friends.

John and Stephanie laugh, listening to my parents tell stories of my childhood. My parents enjoy Stephanie's sense of humor and John's wisdom and wit.

And me?

I'm thankful. Thankful to have such great people in my life who genuinely care for me and about me. Life is good.

Now for the drive back home …

Just like before, John falls asleep in the back seat. I decide to talk to Stephanie about what he told me last week in the bar. I tell her I know she's a lesbian and I'm aware that she likes me. And although I'm not a lesbian myself, I'm happy to continue being her friend if that's okay with her, especially after hearing the sermon we heard today.

I'm a little unsure of what she'll say, but hopeful.

"John has such a big mouth," she says while laughing. "But it's okay, Jenn … I know you're not like me and I know you *don't* like me … At least not like that."

She pauses.

It's quiet for a few seconds. I look over. She's staring out the window.

"Getting to know you has been a real eye-opener. Until you came along, I thought all religious people *hated* my type. But you … You're the first one I've ever met who's treated me like a human being, instead of a target of hate. I cannot tell you how much that means to me."

A tear streams down her left cheek. She takes a deep breath and keeps going.

"These past few months … getting to know you … they have been so much fun. It's actually nice to have a girl *friend* in my life who's not my girlfriend. Know what I mean? It's like you respect me for *who* I am, not *what* I am. And that is rare."

By now I'm crying, too. I consider pulling the car over and giving her a big hug, but just then John lets out a loud snore and

Stephanie and I begin to laugh.

"Ugh! I can't believe I'm crying!" she says, somewhat embarrassed. "What the hell is wrong with me?"

"*You're* crying? Look at me … I'm a mess. I've never had anyone say anything like that to me before. You've been like a big sister to me and I was so afraid to bring all this up – afraid you wouldn't want to be my friend anymore."

Before Stephanie can say anything, John wakes up.

"What's going on with you two? Why are you both crying?"

Stephanie glances over at me, then back at John.

"Oh it's nothing," she says. "Just 'girl talk'."

She looks at me and smiles.

I reach out to her, grabbing her hand.

And I smile back.

The rest of the drive home and the remainder of the school year go as smoothly as the rest of my time at college. The following year, John finishes up at his school while Stephanie graduates from ours. I follow a few years later, graduating with honors.

Although we've all moved on since then and started our own families and careers (it's been nearly 10 years now), the three of us still keep in touch quite often.

John is an assistant professor at a local college. He is married with two children, both of which attend the same preschool as my daughter. I see either of them (John or his wife) every week. He's doing very well.

Stephanie lives about 10 minutes away in a fancy neighborhood. She has a corporate job and a gorgeous home. She recently adopted a little baby boy, and John and I are his godparents!

Lucky me, twice a week "Auntie Jenn" gets to babysit little Sean while Stephanie works. He is adorable.

And as for me ... Well, after graduation, I decided to stay here, in Atlanta. Why? I met the love of my life, Zach! He was introduced to me by John, when they were roommates. Zach and I married shortly after I graduated, and after a few years of babysitting everyone else's kids, we decided to have a few of our own. We now have a beautiful little girl, Carly, and a baby boy on the way. Between volunteering at our church, Zach working full time and me being a stay-at-home mom, we stay quite busy ... and happy.

With all of the updates, I can't help but wonder if you're thinking what I *think* you're thinking. So let me ask and answer your questions for you ...

Is Stephanie still a lesbian?

Yes.

Is John still an atheist?

Yes.

Am I still their friend?

Obviously, *yes.*

Regardless of what the three of us believe concerning lifestyle or religion (or anything else for that matter), one thing we all agree on is that we *can* love and care for each other beyond our differences. We focus on what we *do* have in common, instead of what we don't.

And don't get me wrong – we do have our disagreements. How could we not? But a disagreement with another human being is just that ... a disagreement with another human being. It's not a license to hate that person.

Oil and water ...

At their core – their molecules – they hold properties that keep them from ever mixing with one another. It's just what they do. Yet both *do* exist peacefully, side by side, without ever giving those properties up.

Which brings me back to my pastor's question – the one that started it all …

"*Can* we all just get along?"

To which I reply, "You tell me … Are we not more than oil and water?"

-Jennifer / Atlanta, GA

About The Author

*MJ Wilson is a Self-Help
Author & Speaker*

HOW IT ALL STARTED

A teacher in both public and private schools for 15 years, Wilson came to the conclusion that the biggest problem facing students wasn't academics, but rather, relationships, self-esteem and inspiration. It was at this time he decided to make the world his classroom, rather than his classroom his world. So with an outdated computer and the last penny from his savings, Wilson left his comfortable teaching career behind and set off to fulfill his dream of becoming a best-selling author and inspirational speaker.

CAREER AS AN AUTHOR & SPEAKER

Although first known for his book *The Best College Student Survival Guide Ever Written* (2013), Wilson's first publication actually came long before leaving the teaching profession. He authored *Don't Judge A Bird By Its Color* (2003) – a children's story regarding bullying – with no promotion and, as he puts it, "No idea what I was doing." The book saw meager sales and Wilson returned to the drawing board, somewhat deflated. However, after the success of his college book and several emotional, heart-felt speaking engagements, it was clear to him "You can't teach people if you can't reach people." And from that understanding *Beef Stew for the Mind* was born.

Now, with his career as an author and speaker beginning to flourish, Wilson has already begun work on *Beef Stew for the Mind – Vol. 2* and hopes to make it into a continual series. He also has plans to revamp and re-release *Don't Judge A Bird By Its Color*, as well as author several relationship and dating guides for women. (*And ladies you won't believe what he's writing about next!* The title alone will make some of you blush.)

Finally, he's starting his own YouTube channel, where he'll speak about such topics as relationships, education, and of course, inspiration. (Teachers, you are going to *love* his ideas for reaching students. Stay tuned!)

PERSONAL NOTES
MJ Wilson, who holds a master's degree in education, is also a certified fitness instructor who enjoys music (especially old-school hip-hop), traveling and the occasional karaoke opportunity.

An Ohio native, he now resides in Florida.

For more information about MJ Wilson as an author and speaker, please visit his website or social media platforms.

MJ-Wilson.com

Facebook.com/AuthorMJWilson

AuthorMJWilson

@AuthorMJWilson

Will you help me help others?

Please consider purchasing extra copies of *Beef Stew for the Mind* for one or more of the following:

- **an entrepreneur** in need of inspiration

- **a friend or family member** suffering from depression

- **a single mom** who could use a mental escape or daily break

- **your boss** (and tell him or her to read *Staff Meetings ... Oh How I Hate Thee)*

- **your employees** (it would make a great stocking stuffer!)

- **a local "Book of the Month" club** (and send me their feedback – I'd *love* to hear it!)

- **anyone you can think of who might benefit from reading one or more of these stories** (perhaps someone who's been bullied, divorced, fired, abused or hurt in a relationship.)

When you purchase a copy, you're not only helping me pursue my dream, you're helping others, too. And remember, a portion of the proceeds from *this* book will be used to **help single moms** with everyday living expenses.

Thank you for reading. And thanks for your support.

-MJ Wilson

Acknowledgments

(In no particular order)

Fred Reeder Jr. – Chief Editor and Content Reviewer
Fred has been my best friend since the 5th grade. He is an amazing editor and teacher. Currently a visiting professor at Miami University in Oxford, Ohio, as well as a husband and father of two, for him to edit my book for FREE is *unbelievable*. To say I am grateful to him for what he's done and who he is in my life would be an understatement. I always tell him, "When I make it, *we* make it." And I mean it with all my heart. Fred is truly a *best* friend.

Kirsten Moses – Book Cover Designer and Content Reviewer
Not only a former student of mine, but also my niece, Kirsten is one of the most beautiful people I know. Her personality and creativity are reflected in her work and design, thus making them gorgeous. She not only designed the book cover for *Beef Stew for the Mind*, but also for *The Best College Student Survival Guide Ever Written* and will be doing all of my future cover designs and merchandise as well. She's not just amazing, *she's family* – and that's a beautiful thing.

Kyle Moses – Web Designer
Another former student of mine, and also my niece's husband, Kyle is so good at what he does we often refer to him as "The Jedi" of web design. Everything on my website – *everything* – is because of him and his Jedi powers. He is truly in a class by himself – not just in web design, but in loyalty and character. I am so thankful to not only have him on my team, but to call him family as well. With Kyle, it's "Ride or Die" – and I feel the same. (If you've ever seen any of the *Fast & Furious* movies, you'll understand.)

Alexis Hines – Fitness and Food
Alexis is an up and coming star. She creates and cooks some of the most amazing, healthy meals for all of our team members and reminds us that we need to be in the gym, exercising *daily* – like she does. We're so glad to have her on board with us. Be sure to look for her website and YouTube channel soon. Who knows? I may even collaborate on a healthy food & fitness book with her in the near future. ☺

Kendra Bryant – Photographer (kendramarialee.com)
Kendra, another former student of mine, is such a talented young woman. When I discovered she was doing photography I just had to see her work, and I gotta tell you … I absolutely *loved* it. She has a unique way of capturing the "authentic moment" that typically takes place before the "staged moment" occurs – and that's what sold me. (Who do you think does all my photography now?)

Ashley Watson – Stylist (sistylist.com)
I call her "Miss Wonderful" and yes, I'm going to say it again … *another former student of mine!* Ashley has been styling hair for quite some time and does an amazing job. (What? You think because my head is shaved that I don't have a stylist? Ashley keeps me clean-shaven and looking good all the time.) She is another rising star and I'm so glad I connected with her early. Much like Alexis and Kendra, Ashley's definitely destined for big things.

Tamara Holder – Fashion Extraordinaire (baydiancollection.com)
Are you ready? Say it with me: "Another former student of mine." (Hey, former students are some of the most trustworthy people you'll ever meet!) Tamara, or as I call her, "And 1," is a business entrepreneur and self-starter. Her insight with social media, her connections, and her overall "Get out of my way – I've got things to do" spirit are why she is such an asset to have on my team. (And I haven't even gotten to her fashion expertise! But for the sake of time and space, let's just put it this way: If you want to know where fashion is going, follow Tamara.)

Dr. JoNataye Prather – Speaker/Educator (DrJoNataye.com)
Known to me simply as "Professor," Dr. JoNataye is a rare jewel. (You may recognize her name from our book "*The Best College Student Survival Guide Ever Written*." She wrote the foreword and conducted all the research.) Dr. JoNataye is known for empowering college students to become all they can be, and her story is an inspiration itself. She's been an incredible asset in helping me connect with prominent people, as well as sharing her insight and motivation with me. If you ever get a chance to hear her speak or book her for an event, *do it*. You won't be disappointed.

Scott Wilson – Editor and Content Reviewer
Recognize the last name? Yes, this is my brother. A retired military veteran of 22 years, he served our country well. Now, he's doing the honors of sharing his wisdom and expertise with me, helping create what we believe to be some of the best, most authentic literary work possible. His work ethic and quick turnaround make him a huge asset to my team, and I am grateful. (And just like Fred, he offered his services for FREE! Isn't that wonderful?) I look forward to working with my brother again – especially since I'm trying to convince him to write his own book. (He's practically an expert on leadership and has an entire book finished already – I just gotta get it out of his head first! Stay tuned.)

Stonecreek Dental – Dental Care (helpmysmile.com)
I wish I could say these people are part of "my team," but actually I'm just a loyal customer to *their* team. I've always attended the branch located in Pickerington, Ohio, and let me tell you – this place makes going to the dentist FUN! I want to say THANK YOU to everyone here who has helped to create an experience for me that is pleasant and comfortable. All of you do amazing work and because of it, I now smile confidently. ☺

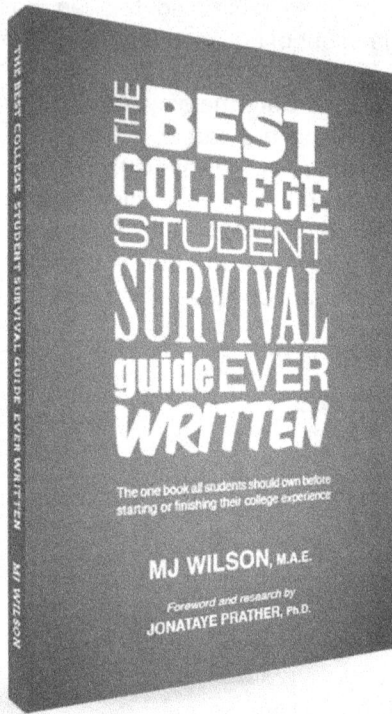

KNOW SOMEONE GOING TO COLLEGE?

In his book *The Best College Student Survival Guide Ever Written*, MJ Wilson explains how to:

- *reduce test stress*
- *choose the right major and school*
- *handle being homesick, lovesick and lonely*
- *deal with difficult professors and impossible exams*
- *keep from changing your major (again and again!)*
- *improve your G.P.A. and graduate on time*
- *leave a legacy and make a grand exit*

"With higher education costs soaring, now more than ever students must choose the best school for them ... and graduate in the quickest amount of time. **Give a gift to a student – or to the student's parents – and help someone save thousands of dollars.**"

-JoNataye Prather, PhD

"I originally thought only students would buy this book, but since its release, **I've sold more copies to the parents of college students than to the students themselves**. It turns out the parents are reading this book first, *before* they give it to their children, ensuring that everyone involved in the college experience is on the same page, wanting the same thing: *a college graduate*. It's a genius idea."

-MJ Wilson, M.A.E.

GIVE A BETTER CHANCE. GIVE A BOOK.

To purchase a copy of *The Best College Student Survival Guide Ever Written* or to request MJ Wilson to speak on your campus, please visit **MJ-Wilson.com**

Got kids?
Know any children
who need a voice, too?

DON'T JUDGE A BIRD BY ITS COLOR

MJ WILSON
CHILDREN'S BOOK
SPRING 2016

www.ingramcontent.com/pod-product-compliance
Lightning Source LLC
LaVergne TN
LVHW051347080426
835509LV00020BA/3326